Absolute Faith!

Trevor Newport

New Wine Press

New Wine Press
PO Box 17
Chichester
England PO20 6YB

ISBN: 1 874367 99 X

Typeset by CRB Associates, Reepham, Norfolk.
Printed in England by Clays Ltd, St Ives plc.

Contents

Chapter 1

Introduction

I had been a Christian for about a year when a visiting speaker came to our church and spoke for four nights on the subject of faith. If you had asked me before he came if I knew much about faith I probably would have said yes. However, I soon realised that I knew very little about faith or how to use it. This prompted a quest in me to find out everything I could about faith, because it was fundamental to the Christian life.

> *'For whatsoever is born of God overcometh the world: and this is the victory that overcometh the world, even our faith.'*
> (1 John 5:4)

The preacher said that every Christian was a world over-comer and that it was only through faith that we could do this. I looked up everything I could about faith because I wanted to be a world overcomer. I did not want to be overcome all the time by problems that the world threw at me.

Fortunately cassette tapes had been made of the four meetings with this great speaker and so I bought these tapes and nearly wore them out over the next few months. I realised that each time I listened to them I would hear something new. It was awesome. It was as if he did not say it the first time, which sounds silly, but that is what it was like for me. I later realised that this was called revelation.

> *'For therein is the righteousness of God revealed from faith to faith: as it is written, The just shall live by faith.'*
> (Romans 1:17)

Thus faith is a revelation which keeps growing as we use it and meditate on God's Word. I pray that as you read this book a thirst will develop in your heart to grow in understanding of faith and how to apply it to every circumstance in life. You will never be the same again once you know how to use your faith.

You may be saying to yourself right now that you have been a Christian for a long time and therefore must have a lot of faith. Sadly, this is often not the case. I see it all the time. As soon as someone gets their back against the wall they simply do not know what to do. After you have read this book you should have a clear understanding how to get out of situations that the world and the devil throw at us.

Take a look at this verse of Scripture:

> *'But without faith it is impossible to please him: for he that cometh to God must believe that he is, and that he is a rewarder of them that diligently seek him.'* (Hebrews 11:6)

We need to develop our faith to the point where we have a total trust in God, knowing that He will answer us and come to our help, whatever the situation.

Prepare for your whole relationship with God to undergo a complete overhaul as you enter the faith realm where so few seem to enter.

Chapter 2

Where Does Faith Come From?

Romans 10:17 says,

> *'So then faith cometh by hearing, and hearing by the word of God.'*

If someone that you trust says something to you, then you will usually believe them because they are reliable. This is how faith works in simple terms. If someone says to you that they will meet you at a certain place and time then you will **act on their word** and meet them. You have put your faith in that person's word. You heard a piece of information and acted on it. This is what faith is.

God has made many statements in His precious Word that He expects us to act upon and see results. As you read and understand His Word then you need to act on what He says.

James 1:22 says,

> *'But be ye doers of the word, and not hearers only, deceiving your own selves.'*

Don't just hear what God says and then do nothing about it! Once we know what His Word says then we have an awesome responsibility to do what it says.

The Reliability of the Source!

It is so important to establish exactly **who said it**!

Imagine that you were in church one Sunday morning and a drunken man walked into the meeting and said that there was a bomb in the church which would go off in about five minutes. But if you knew that this same drunken man had said the same thing every week for a month his word would not produce much faith in you, would it?

Now consider the most reliable person that you know coming into your church one Sunday morning and saying the same thing! It would change matters a lot! Thus the same message produces two opposite results. Therefore the source of information that you are seeking to act upon is of the utmost importance!

I know that the most reliable and dependable person to me is my wife and if she said anything to me I would believe it without seeking confirmation, because I know that she is absolutely trustworthy and totally honest.

This is how we need to be when it comes to God's Word, the Bible. **The Lord is the most trustworthy Person you will *ever* meet!** Everyone else fades into insignificance compared with Him. Hallelujah! When He says anything about any subject then He means it.

Thus faith does not just come by hearing information, it comes by hearing facts from a reliable source. Therefore, before you act on anything always make sure that you have checked the source from which it came. In fact this is true about everything in life! When it comes to grey areas in life people will often shop around for their information before making their decisions. I am glad that we do not have to shop around for our information when it comes to the Word of God. The Word of God needs no confirmation at all. What it says is what it means and that is final. For instance, when God says,

> *'If we confess our sins, he is faithful and just to forgive us our sins, and to cleanse us from all unrighteousness,'*
>
> (1 John 1:9)

all we have to do is to believe it absolutely. Once you have confessed your sin to God then you know that He will forgive you and cleanse you from it. This is how faith for anything works.

> *'Sanctify them through thy truth: **thy word is truth.**'*
>
> (John 17:17)

This is a simple truth and yet very profound.

I believe that one of the reasons why many find this very hard to come to terms with is that they have been let down by human beings too often, and so when God says something they cannot relate to His absolute integrity. If we are going to understand our tremendous faith in God then we are going to have to come to the place of accepting the Word of God as the **truth**.

> *'Jesus saith unto him, **I am the way, the truth, and the life:** no man cometh unto the Father, but by me.'*
>
> (John 14:6)

Jesus doesn't just tell the truth, **He *is* the Truth**!

This means that all that He ever says is true. In fact, because He is the **truth** itself, it means that God does not have the capacity to lie to us. This is something that we can do that God **cannot** do. We can tell lies and pervert the truth but God is limited in this respect. He cannot sin, He cannot lie and He cannot deceive you in any way!

This is awesome, particularly when your confidence in people has been shattered. People let us down and make false promises to us. This happens to me also! I have had many people make promises to me and then turn around and break their word.

I can testify that after nearly 20 years of serving the Lord, He has never deceived me or lied to me. Everything He has said has come to pass. I have put all my trust in His wonderful Word and I have never found His Word to be wrong. If it seems not to be working then the problem is not with God but me. We will look into this in more detail in a later chapter.

Numbers 23:19 says,

> '*God is not a man, that he should lie; neither the son of man, that he should repent: hath he said, and shall he not do it? or hath he spoken, and shall he not make it good?*'

This sums up exactly what I am saying here.

I want to share a testimony at this point to encourage you to pursue faith in God for the rest of your life. The Lord spoke to my heart a few years ago and told me to go to Argentina. He does this regularly to me and I have visited about 40 countries in the last five years by faith. I did not know anyone in Argentina but was prepared to simply board a plane and go. My faith in God is such that I will go anywhere that He sends me.

I was preaching in America and happened to mention to a friend that I was going to Argentina the next year. He said that he knew someone there and he made contact with them to let them know that I was going. I booked my flight with the only money that I had and was preparing to go.

On the Friday before I was due to leave on the Monday, I telephoned the church where I had made contact to see if they had received my letter and my friend's letter of recommendation. They had but said that it was not convenient for me to come at this time and would I please cancel my flight and come later in the year. I could not do this since my ticket was paid for and no refunds were given. I replied that I would be coming whatever they said. When God speaks and commands me to go then I go whatever man may say!

They insisted that I should not go because they already had visiting speakers booked and there would be nothing for them to open up for me. I told them I would be arriving on the Tuesday morning whether they had anything for me or not. They then asked me if they could do anything for me. I simply requested that they pick me up at the airport, put me into a hotel and then leave me. I told them not to be overconcerned about me since God would look after me.

After I came off the telephone it looked like I had got it wrong in the natural and that I would have nowhere to speak. I assumed that the Lord did not want me to speak with that group of churches and that He would open another door.

I boarded the plane for Frankfurt and then connected with Buenos Aires. When I arrived I did not know if anyone would be there to meet me or not. I was prepared for both! I went into the Arrival Lounge where everybody was waiting to pick up passengers and I looked for my name on all the boards. They were all in Spanish and I quickly scanned them for my name. I could not see it anywhere and was just about to go through the door when I saw a sign saying 'TREVOR NEWPORT'. One of the pastors was holding it up right by the door and so I went up to him. He introduced himself to me and welcomed me to Argentina. He was a bit suspicious of me and asked me many questions.

He took me to a hotel and then said to me, 'We have arranged for you to preach many times while you are with us!' I was pleasantly surprised and went to my room and thanked God for His faithfulness.

I spent the first two days praying and fasting and then had a busy preaching schedule. I also wrote a large portion of one of my books while in the hotel during the day. I never waste time when I am abroad. I always have my laptop with me ready to write my next book. I cannot stand having nothing to do all day. I am a very active person.

They had me preaching in Buenos Aires and then flew me to Cordoba. I then flew to Rosario, and then we drove back to Buenos Aires. I was speaking in the largest churches I had ever seen before and loved every minute of it. Many people were born again, hundreds baptised in the Holy Spirit, scores of people delivered from demons and hundreds healed of all kinds of things. It was one of the highlights of my ministry.

Anyway, I was staying in a three star hotel in Buenos Aires

and assumed that the church would cover my expenses. I had very little money with me and no credit cards. Thus I had no way of paying for my hotel bill at all.

On the Thursday morning of the second week (I was due to fly home on the Sunday morning after church) the telephone rang in my room. It was the church where I was preaching. It was actually the senior apostle's daughter who could speak good English. She asked me if I was able to pay my hotel bill. I said that I could and that the Lord would provide for me! This was a statement of faith since I did not have the money but was in faith for it – I was assuming that the church would pay for it! She then said that she was pleased that I was alright because she was ringing me to tell me that the church had no spare money and therefore was not able to pay my hotel bill for me. I was not moved by this because if God had sent me there then He would provide for me!

Two hours later the telephone rang again. The voice on the other end was American. It was a man who had heard me speak the week before and wanted to see me. He took me out for a meal along with his wife and asked for some advice which I gave him through a prophetic word.

He then told me that he wanted to give me some money! God had spoken to him to pay my air fare! He did not know how much it was and so he had prayed and he gave me $1030. My air fare was $1029. Praise God. He gave it to me in cash which meant that I could pay the hotel room! He then asked me if I had any books left. I had taken 200 books with me since God had told me to do so. However, nobody could read them in South America since they all speak Spanish! I felt silly carrying all my books around with me and thought that I had got it wrong again. He wanted to buy 200 books off me and paid me in cash!

I then went to a church that gave me $300 and as I was leaving I was given $600 by the church that had not had any money before! I left the country with $4500 in cash. I had not told a single person about my situation but had simply left it with the Lord.

Philippians 4:19 says:

> *'But my God shall supply all your need according to his riches in glory by Christ Jesus.'*

I have had to put my complete trust in this verse many times and God has never let me down!

This kind of faith does not develop overnight but comes in stages:

> *'For therein is the righteousness of God revealed **from faith to faith**: as it is written, The just shall live by faith.'*
>
> (Romans 1:17)

Our faith grows one step at a time so that we can take on bigger and bigger challenges for His glory.

If the Lord had told me to do the kind of things that I am doing now 10 years ago, I would have collapsed in a heap! My faith has had to develop in stages so do not think that God will call upon you to do anything like I am talking about yet. But one day, who knows what you might be doing in His name?

I have shared this testimony with you to whet your appetite to seek to have this kind of faith yourself. You may never have to do these kinds of daring exploits but may have to demonstrate faith in another way. Who knows what you may be called upon to do? We just have to take each step as God gives it to us. I used to read books about people doing mighty things for God and taking huge steps of faith and I can remember thinking that I could never see myself doing anything like that. However, now that my faith has grown over the years I am doing things that I once thought were for others only.

> *'The steps of a good man are ordered by the LORD: and he delighteth in his way.'*
>
> (Psalm 37:23)

Take all the steps that He gives you and just watch your faith grow and grow.

Chapter 3

What Is Faith?

This may seem a silly question but I have asked it for two reasons. Firstly, because so many 'mature' believers don't appear to understand it and, secondly, the Bible gives us a clear definition as to what faith is. Hebrews 11:1 says,

> 'Now faith is the substance of things hoped for, the evidence of things not seen.'

The last phrase of this verse which reads 'the evidence of things not seen' can be translated equally as 'the evidence of things not yet revealed to the physical senses'. Verse 6 of the same passage says that we cannot please God without faith. Therefore, we need to be accurate as to what faith is before we can start acting upon it!

What Faith Isn't

John Wesley said that the Church had accepted Satan's counterfeit for faith, something that sounded like faith to the point where many could not tell the difference. This counterfeit was called 'Mental assent'. In other words simply agreeing with the Bible only, but never ever acting upon it. The Word of God was written to give you victory over the devil, the flesh and the world, but if you never act on what it says then it will never do you any good.

You may be wondering what I am talking about. I am going to be very careful not to assume too much, which I often do. I have often assumed that those I am speaking to understand more than they do. I have been very surprised that this message of faith is one of the most misunderstood subjects in the Christian life and yet it is probably the most important. Everything else works because of our faith in and towards God, so I am going to make sure that I do not gloss over any of my points. Even if you think that you know everything about faith, then please read the whole book carefully. Thank you!

Thus, faith is simply hearing and acting upon what God has said. This is true about the written Word of God or the spoken Word of God. These are called the general will of God and the specific will of God. The written Word of God, when acted upon, will cause you to know and understand the general will of God for your life. Then when you are firmly living in the general will of God, He can then speak to you directly by means of the Holy Spirit about His specific will for your life, for instance, your calling in the Body of Christ. Sadly, many Christians never give themselves a chance to find the specific will of God for their lives because they never apply the written Word to their everyday life. This is such a shame, because it can only produce a very low level of spiritual existence, which causes sadness, sorrow and continual defeat. All the devil needs to do with such Christians is to arrange a set of difficult circumstances and they fall every time. This is not God's best for you at all! God has a much better existence for you.

Hebrews 10:38 says,

'Now the just shall live by faith: but if any man draw back, my soul shall have no pleasure in him.'

What a statement! In other words, if we do not live by faith then God Himself will have no pleasure in us! He means it! Living by faith is actually not an option, it is a command. The Lord virtually takes it for granted that His people will live

by faith and not sight. I want us to look at one of the greatest
men of faith that has ever lived. Prepare to be rebuked!

Noah

Let me give you some amazing facts about his circumstances.
Noah had no Bible to stir his faith. Think about that for a
moment! He had no church to go to and ask questions about
faith etc. He had no pastor to quiz about spiritual things. He
had no mentor at all. He had no examples of faith to read
about to encourage him. He was not born again or filled with
the Holy Spirit! On top of all that ... **it had never rained
upon the earth before**! All Noah had was one word from
God.

> *'And God said unto Noah, The end of all flesh is come
> before me; for the earth is filled with violence through them;
> and, behold, I will destroy them with the earth.'*
> (Genesis 6:13)

> *'Make thee an ark of gopher wood; rooms shalt thou make in
> the ark, and shalt pitch it within and without with pitch.'*
> (Genesis 6:14)

Noah had to build a huge boat the size of a World War II
battleship with only three men and four women! No wonder
it took about 90 years to build it! All that time there was
never any sign of rain. What faith! Then came the time for
the animals to enter the ark. Just picture it for a moment!
How do you persuade two lions for instance to come with
you and get into a big boat! Imagine rounding up two
giraffes! I can't even imagine what it must have been like
when it came to cobras, pythons, birds, elephants etc. It is so
awesome. The other people must have thought he was mad!
It was a very corrupt society and so they would constantly
have made fun of him and his family. He was a preacher of
righteousness and yet did not see any converts! And still it
did not rain. Oh, what faith! Noah puts us all to shame!

The day came when God called Noah and his family into the ark and the doors were shut. The whole world perished in the water flood that followed, but eight faithful ones were saved!

Noah was just one man who believed the Word of God. Make a decision today to become a real believer in what God says and stop playing at Christianity! Spend some time just meditating on the life of Noah and what he did. You will find yourself repenting of unbelief and complacency before you know it!

I Will Believe it When I See it!

This is often what the world says. It is the classic statement of unbelief. Many people say this about God. They say that they will believe in Him if they can see Him. This is the opposite of faith.

There was once a queen who had been told about the wisdom and wealth of a man named Solomon. She had been told about everything that he had, but she did not believe it until she had seen it for herself. This is a good example of how unbelief operates.

> *'And when the queen of Sheba heard of the fame of Solomon concerning the name of the LORD, she came to prove him with hard questions. And she came to Jerusalem with a very great train, with camels that bare spices, and very much gold, and precious stones: and when she was come to Solomon, she communed with him of all that was in her heart. And Solomon told her all her questions: there was not any thing hid from the king, which he told her not. And when the queen of Sheba had seen all Solomon's wisdom, and the house that he had built, And the meat of his table, and the sitting of his servants, and the attendance of his ministers, and their apparel, and his cupbearers, and his ascent by which he went up unto the house of the LORD; there was no more spirit in her.*

> *And she said to the king, It was a true report that I heard*
> *in mine own land of thy acts and of thy wisdom.* **Howbeit I**
> **believed not the words, until I came, and mine eyes**
> **had seen it: and, behold, the half was not told me: thy**
> **wisdom and prosperity exceedeth the fame which I**
> **heard.'**   (1 Kings 10:1–7)

She only believed when she had seen it for herself. Jesus
also had to deal with this same kind of spirit in the gospels
with a famous man called Thomas. In fact he was made
famous because of his unbelief!

> 'Then saith he to Thomas, Reach hither thy finger, and
> behold my hands; and reach hither thy hand, and thrust it
> into my side: and **be not faithless, but believing.** And
> Thomas answered and said unto him, My Lord and my God.
> **Jesus saith unto him, Thomas, because thou hast seen**
> **me, thou hast believed: blessed are they that have not**
> **seen, and yet have believed.'**   (John 20:27–29)

This is a wonderful story in itself, because Jesus takes His
valuable time to minister to Thomas. He could have just
written him off but He didn't. He gave him a chance to
change from a heart of unbelief to having a heart of faith. I
always marvel how Jesus went straight up to him and
confronted him before doing anything else. Jesus knew how
important it was to have a unity of faith amongst His
followers and so He wanted to bring Thomas up to the rest
of them. It is worth looking at what Thomas had said just
prior to this incident rather than simply moving on:

> 'But Thomas, one of the twelve, called Didymus, was not
> with them when Jesus came. **The other disciples therefore**
> **said unto him, We have seen the Lord. But he said**
> **unto them, Except I shall see in his hands the print of**
> **the nails, and put my finger into the print of the nails,**
> **and thrust my hand into his side, I will not believe.'**
>   (John 20:24–25)

It is interesting that even though these men were Thomas's closest friends, who had spent so much time with each other and Jesus Christ, yet he still did not believe them. This was the most reliable source that Thomas could have had regarding seeing Jesus and yet he was still so grounded in unbelief that nothing short of Jesus Himself confronting him would show him otherwise. We all look at Thomas, and probably many of us have even had a bad attitude towards this poor man, and yet we have all done similar things, but nobody was around to see us! Check out your own unbelief before criticising him. When we are faced with difficult circumstances I wonder how our faith stands up to severe testing.

It is often when our faith is tried that we really know how much trust we really have in the Lord. 1 Peter 1:7 says,

'That the trial of your faith, being much more precious than of gold that perisheth, though it be tried with fire, might be found unto praise and honour and glory at the appearing of Jesus Christ.'

Chapter 4

How Faith Really Works

Read through the following scriptures:

> *'So then faith cometh by hearing, and hearing by the word of God.'*   (Romans 10:17)

> *'And Jesus answering saith unto them, Have faith in God.* **For verily I say unto you, That whosoever shall say unto this mountain, Be thou removed, and be thou cast into the sea; and shall not doubt in his heart, but shall believe that those things which he saith shall come to pass; he shall have whatsoever he saith. Therefore I say unto you, What things soever ye desire, when ye pray, believe that ye receive them, and ye shall have them.'**   (Mark 11:22–24)

> *'We having the same spirit of faith, according as it is written,* **I believed, and therefore have I spoken; we also believe, and therefore speak.'**   (2 Corinthians 4:13)

Faith has to be in two places before it can really work. In our heart and then our mouth:

> *'But what saith it?* **The word is nigh thee, even in thy mouth, and in thy heart:** *that is, the word of faith, which we preach; That if thou shalt confess with thy mouth the*

> *Lord Jesus, and shalt believe in thine heart that God hath
> raised him from the dead, thou shalt be saved. For with
> the **heart** man believeth unto righteousness; and with the
> **mouth** confession is made unto salvation.'*

(Romans 10:8–10)

This is how faith works. We believe in our heart and then
confess it with our mouth. That is why we need to be verbal
in our testimony about our salvation as well as simply
believing in our heart. I have had people say to me that their
faith is in their heart and that is good enough. Not according
to the Scriptures! The vocal part of our faith is just as
important as believing in our heart.

It is a true fact of life that we speak out what we believe.
'I've always believed that' is a familiar phrase by many. Even
if it is wrong they still believe it. Why? It is simply that they
heard something years ago and have always believed it.
When I first heard about the gospel message I would never
allow the Bible to be read out loud, simply because I heard
from someone when I was a small boy that the Bible was full
of contradictions and could not be trusted. I was believing a
lie with all of my heart and it affected me greatly. Satan uses
this all the time to keep people from the truth. In fact it
wasn't until after I was born again that I realised that I had
been deceived all those years before, and it had held me in
bondage.

In the light of this we need to make sure that what we are
believing is correct! Unfortunately, since many of us have
spent much of life outside of the Christian faith, we have
built up a huge mass of wrong thinking and thus wrong
believing. When we become Christians we have a lot of
relearning to do! I certainly did. I slowly realised that most
of the things that I had been brought up to believe were
wrong when it came to spiritual things. I had many religious
ideas that I had simply picked up along the way, because
people whom I respected said them. Then when I started to
study the Word of God for myself I was shocked to find out
just how much I didn't know! This is why, if we are to grow

in faith, we need to spend much quality time reading the Bible and meditating on its wonderful truths. This is where your faith will really grow.

> *'All scripture is given by inspiration of God, and is profitable for doctrine, for reproof, for correction, for instruction in righteousness: That the man of God may be perfect, thoroughly furnished unto all good works.'*
>
> (2 Timothy 3:16–17)

> *'For the word of God is quick, and powerful, and sharper than any twoedged sword, piercing even to the dividing asunder of soul and spirit, and of the joints and marrow, and is a discerner of the thoughts and intents of the heart.'*
>
> (Hebrews 4:12)

> *'Thy word have I hid in mine heart, that I might not sin against thee.'* (Psalm 119:11)

When I first came into the ministry I was pastoring a small church in Liverpool. I spent about eight hours a day studying the Bible for about two years. This was the best training ground I could have had. My faith grew so much during that time. I was fasting at least two days a week and spending much time in prayer also.

So many people want to develop strong faith and do great things for God but are not prepared to pay the price. Make a start today by spending much quality time in the Bible. You will never regret any time spent with God in His Word. It is self-revealing. The Holy Spirit will be able to show you things as you soak up the Old and New Testaments. Don't just read the New Testament. You will miss out on so much by reading only the parts that you like! Read it all and then the Holy Spirit will be able to bring it back to your memory. This happens all the time to me now. Since I have spent so much time in the Bible I will be going about my life, and all of a sudden a verse of Scripture will come into my mind, and it will be perfect for the situation that I am in. It happens all the time. It is wonderful. However, if I had not read the Word of God so much, then this would not happen! It only happens because I have done my part.

Examine how much time you spend doing other things and make some quality changes. Many people spend far too much time in front of the **television** each night when they could be reading the Word and praying. Your life will never be the same once you start to take spiritual things seriously. It takes discipline to make these kind of changes but it is worth it for all eternity!

How Does Faith Get Into Our Heart?

First of all it begins with the mind! The mind is often ignored when we discuss spiritual things, but it is essential that we examine its part with regard to faith.

> *'And be not conformed to this world: but be ye transformed by the renewing of your mind, that ye may prove what is that good, and acceptable, and perfect, will of God.'*
>
> (Romans 12:2)

> *'For who hath known the mind of the Lord, that he may instruct him? But we have the mind of Christ.'*
>
> (1 Corinthians 2:16)

> *'And he that searcheth the hearts knoweth what is the mind of the Spirit, because he maketh intercession for the saints according to the will of God.'* (Romans 8:27)

The mind is the first place that we all assess things before we can ever believe them. It is no use saying to someone 'believe it in your heart', if they have not even thought about it in their mind. It is absurd in fact to think that we can somehow bypass our mind! Thus, whenever we hear of a new truth from God's Word we are supposed to think about it first in our mind. Once we have thought it through we can then start to believe it with our heart.

> *'For unto us was the gospel preached, as well as unto them:*
> *but the word preached did not profit them, not being mixed*
> *with faith in them that heard it.'*   (Hebrews 4:2)

Once you have heard the truth about anything you then have to release your faith from your heart (or spirit) before it will change your situation. Once this process has been reached we can then confess what we believe with absolute confidence.

I personally think that this is where many people have missed the wonderful truth concerning the true teaching of faith. People have tried to confess the Word simply from their mind but they have no foundation in their heart. You have to believe with all your heart before faith will work. This is where teaching is so desperately needed in the Body of Christ. Unfortunately, some people get a hold of just a few facts and then try to act on part of a truth instead of getting the whole message. This is why many are going around today and saying that 'it doesn't work'. I like what one person says when things don't appear to be working. They said 'well you don't know enough'. This is often the case. Look at this verse:

> *'My people are destroyed for lack of knowledge: because*
> *thou hast rejected knowledge, I will also reject thee, that thou*
> *shalt be no priest to me: seeing thou hast forgotten the law of*
> *thy God, I will also forget thy children.'*   (Hosea 4:6)

Make sure that you know all the facts before you act on the Word and then you can be assured of great results! One of the reasons why people don't receive anything from God is ignorance regarding the nature of God. God loves everyone with the same love and gives the same attention to us all:

> *'For there is no respect of persons with God.'*
> (Romans 2:11)

This is so important. I was praying for a wonderful old gentleman last night who had been a believer for many

decades. His eyesight was going and I asked him if he had
faith for God to heal him now. He said that he could believe
for others but not himself. This is ignorance of the Word of
God. God will do the same for one as He does for the other.
We need to understand this truth. Look at what the Bible
says about salvation:

> *'Who will have all men to be saved, and to come unto*
> *the knowledge of the truth.'*   (1 Timothy 2:4)

Even though it is the will of God for all men to be saved it
does not mean that they all will. It is the same in the
Christian Church today; just because it is God's will for all
to be healed there are still some who are not. This is not
God's fault at all but simply our ignorance of the truth of the
Word of God.

Another point to remember about faith is that it will only
develop as we use it. Once we have faith in a particular aspect
of God's Word then we need to act upon that revelation and
we then become established in that aspect. Once we have
become established in a truth we then pass from the state of
believing to **knowing**. I know that healing works. I know
that prosperity works. I know that deliverance works etc.
I have stood on the Word of God in all these areas of life and
have proved again and again that they all work. If something
does not seem to be working then I know that it is me who is
wrong and not God. If I have done all that I know to do
about something and have been standing for a while and it
still does not look as if it is working then I will spend some
time seeking God about it to see where I have got it wrong. I
never say or even think that God is wrong or His promises are
failing. I take full responsibility myself and after a season of
prayer and fasting I know that the answer will come. This is
where the Holy Spirit comes into effect. We need to become
sensitive to the Holy Spirit as well as standing on the Word of
God. However, the Holy Spirit will never contradict the
Scriptures but will always complement them. If ever you
hear a word from what you think is the Holy Spirit and it

does not come in line with the written Word of God then **always** reject it. The Word and the Holy Spirit always agree! Praise God.

Chapter 5

The Trying of Your Faith

Once you begin to understand the principles of faith in God's Word you will encounter Satan as never before. The enemy does not want you to become established in the Word of God and so will try everything in his arsenal to prevent you from growing up in faith. His greatest victory comes when you say that it works for some but not for others and become discouraged.

The story of the seed and the sower gives us a real warning of how the enemy comes along:

> 'The sower soweth the word. **And these are they by the way side, where the word is sown; but when they have heard, Satan cometh immediately, and taketh away the word that was sown in their hearts.**
>
> And these are they likewise which are sown on stony ground; who, when they have heard the word, immediately receive it with gladness; And have no root in themselves, and **so endure but for a time: afterward, when affliction or persecution ariseth for the word's sake, immediately they are offended.**
>
> And these are they which are sown among thorns; such as hear the word, **And the cares of this world, and the deceitfulness of riches, and the lusts of other things entering in, choke the word, and it becometh unfruitful.**

> *And these are they which are sown on good ground; such*
> *as hear the word, and receive it, and bring forth fruit, some*
> *thirtyfold, some sixty, and some an hundred.'*
>
> (Mark 4:14–20)

Satan wants to steal the Word out of your heart as quickly as he can because he knows that once it becomes established in you he is going to get a continual sore head!

Satan uses many tactics to try to steal the Word from young believers. He will try well-meaning, unbelieving Christians who tried using their faith years ago and failed and will tell you not to try. Books will also help to lead a life of defeat and misery since there are many books written by sincere Christians that tell you why it doesn't work! Be careful who you listen to and what you read. I advise you to make the Word of God your main source of reading before any books about anything, including my books! If the books that you read do not point you back to God's Word then stop reading them. His Word is final!

Patience

> *'Knowing this, that the trying of your faith worketh patience.*
> *But let patience have her perfect work, that ye may be perfect*
> *and entire, wanting nothing.'*   (James 1:3–4)

One of the things that you are going to have to learn is patience. When you come to this great subject of faith it is coupled with many things. To see the promises of God work for your benefit by using the principles of faith you need to learn that time is involved. From the moment that you pray in faith about something a process begins. I believe that angels are released to start to bring about the answer to your prayer. If you become discouraged before the manifestation happens then the angels will stop and wait for you to get back onto your faith. I thank God that even though we stumble we can always get up again!

'Rejoice not against me, O mine enemy: when I fall, I shall arise; when I sit in darkness, the LORD shall be a light unto me. I will bear the indignation of the LORD, because I have sinned against him, until he plead my cause, and execute judgement for me: he will bring me forth to the light, and I shall behold his righteousness.'*   (Micah 7:8–9)

The Lord is more lenient with effort than He is with laziness and lethargy. He comes to the aid of those who are making an attempt. Lazy people do not get very far with spiritual things. Diligence is a vital part of faith!

'He becometh poor that dealeth with a slack hand: but the hand of the diligent maketh rich.'   (Proverbs 10:4)

'The hand of the diligent shall bear rule: but the slothful shall be under tribute.'   (Proverbs 12:24)

'The thoughts of the diligent tend only to plenteousness; but of every one that is hasty only to want.'   (Proverbs 21:5)

Patient people are winners! Look at some of the Old Testament giants whom we esteem highly because of their great successes. Noah waited patiently for about 90 years before God's promise worked. Abraham waited 29 years before Sarah became pregnant. David waited years after being anointed by Samuel before finally becoming king. If you are an impatient person then you are going to have to change in this area if you are going to see any real results in this life. I have had to become patient over the years. I have often thought that things should have moved a lot faster than they have, but I have learned over the years that patience has great power.

'For whatsoever things were written aforetime were written for our learning, that we through patience and comfort of the scriptures might have hope. Now the God of patience and

> *consolation grant you to be likeminded one toward another*
> *according to Christ Jesus.'*   · (Romans 15:4–5)

> *'Truly the signs of an apostle were wrought among you in all*
> *patience, in signs, and wonders, and mighty deeds.'*
>   (2 Corinthians 12:12)

> *'Strengthened with all might, according to his glorious power,*
> *unto all patience and longsuffering with joyfulness.'*
>   (Colossians 1:11)

> *'So that we ourselves glory in you in the churches of God for*
> *your patience and faith in all your persecutions and tribula-*
> *tions that ye endure.'*   (2 Thessalonians 1:4)

> *'That ye be not slothful, but followers of them who through*
> *faith and patience inherit the promises.'*   (Hebrews 6:12)

You will notice how often patience is mentioned with
faith. Paul had learned that when you walk with God by faith
then patience has to be a major part of it.

> *'But speaking the truth in love, may grow up into him in all*
> *things, which is the head, even Christ.'*   (Ephesians 4:15)

This verse brings us to another important aspect of faith . . .
which is **love**.

> *'For in Jesus Christ neither circumcision availeth any thing,*
> *nor uncircumcision; but faith **which worketh by love**.'*
>   (Galatians 5:6)

Faith can only operate when it is motivated by love! Love
for God and love for people. Also, one thing that is essential
is that we prove our love to God by obeying Him!

> *'For this is the love of God, that we keep his commandments:*
> ***and his commandments are not grievous.'***   (1 John 5:3)

This means that we do things His way and not our way.

> *'In all thy ways acknowledge him, and he shall direct thy paths.'* (Proverbs 3:6)

I have determined in my life that I am going to serve Him and obey Him for the rest of my life. I have also learned that the only way to do this is by faith and by observing all His commandments to me.

Another ingredient for faith to work is **joy**. Faith is not a mere mechanical exercise that we do every day but an absolute joy. One person once said that faith was like dynamite but joy was the fuse! Joy ignites our faith and causes it to work! No wonder that Paul was always exorting us to rejoice at all times. He knew the power of joy in the face of much opposition!

> *'Be glad in the Lord, and rejoice, ye righteous: and shout for joy, all ye that are upright in heart.'* (Psalm 32:11)

> *'Hitherto have ye asked nothing in my name: ask, and ye shall receive, that your joy may be full.'* (John 16:24)

> *'Now the God of hope fill you with all joy and peace in believing, that ye may abound in hope, through the power of the Holy Ghost.'* (Romans 15:13)

> *'Not for that we have dominion over your faith, but are helpers of your joy: for by faith ye stand.'*
> (2 Corinthians 1:24)

> *'And having this confidence, I know that I shall abide and continue with you all for your furtherance and **joy of faith**.'*
> (Philippians 1:25)

Thus when you are standing in faith for something you need to be patient, motivated by love and full of joy in eager anticipation of its complete fulfilment!

One of the reasons why joy and praise are so important is that they deal with the enemy! They are powerful weapons for us to use to ward off the devil's attacks against our stand of faith.

Chapter 6

How to Pray in Faith

I want to say something which is absolutely vital before we can even start to pray about anything. Before we can release any prayer up to the Throne Room we need to first establish that it is God's will for us to have what we are asking for!

1 John 5:14–15 says,

> *'And this is the confidence that we have in him, that, if we ask any thing according to his will, he heareth us. And if we know that he hears us, whatsoever we ask, we know that we have the petitions that we desired of him.'*

When I read these verses many years ago I realised that the reason why many people do not get their prayers answered is that they do not even get past the first hurdle. If it is not the Father's will then you cannot change His mind!

There are two aspects to knowing the will of God to enable us to pray in faith. Firstly, the written Word of God is the will of God. Therefore, if something that you desire is in the Word of God then you can **always** pray in faith for it! For example, healing is all the way through the Scriptures and so it is always His **will** to heal you:

> *'And said, If thou wilt diligently hearken to the voice of the LORD thy God, and wilt do that which is right in his sight, and wilt give ear to his commandments, and keep all his*

statutes, I will put none of these diseases upon thee, which I have brought upon the Egyptians: **for I am the LORD that healeth thee.'** (Exodus 15:26)

'Who forgiveth all thine iniquities; who healeth all thy diseases.' (Psalm 103:3)

'He healeth the broken in heart, and bindeth up their wounds.' (Psalm 147:3)

'He sent his word, and healed them, and delivered them from their destructions.' (Psalm 107:20)

'But he was wounded for our transgressions, he was bruised for our iniquities: the chastisement of our peace was upon him; **and with his stripes we are healed.'**
(Isaiah 53:5)

'And Jesus went about all Galilee, teaching in their synagogues, and preaching the gospel of the kingdom, and **healing all manner of sickness and all manner of disease** among the people. And his fame went throughout all Syria: and they brought unto him all sick people that were taken with divers diseases and torments, and those which were possessed with devils, and those which were lunatick, and those that had the palsy; **and he healed them.'**
(Matthew 4:23–24)

'And he healed many that were sick of divers diseases, and cast out many devils; and suffered not the devils to speak, because they knew him.' (Mark 1:34)

'And the people, when they knew it, followed him: and he received them, and spake unto them of the kingdom of God, **and healed them that had need of healing.'**
(Luke 9:11)

> '*Who his own self bare our sins in his own body on the tree,*
> *that we, being dead to sins, should live unto righteousness:*
> ***by whose stripes ye were healed.*'*   (1 Peter 2:24)

Whenever I am praying for someone to be healed I never have to pray first to see if it is the will of God to heal that person. I know it is the will of God to heal. However, the healing power of God is sometimes held back because of sin, rebellion, unbelief, spirits of infirmity, hereditary bondages, unforgiveness etc. This is where teaching is so important on all these subjects. One thing is certain, there is never anything wrong with the power of God! If sickness attacks my body then I always do a check to see if I have allowed the enemy in to place such a sickness on me. I have to confess that it is usually my fault if sickness gets a hold over me. Sometimes it is just the enemy trying to get me to accept something and I know that I must exercise my authority in the name of Jesus Christ to combat such an attack. (My next book is going to be on the subject of healing and so I will not be answering all your questions and concerns in this book, but please be patient for the next one!)

Thus, if the Bible tells you something that you can ask for, then you do not need any other confirmation. Praise God for the Word of God.

The second aspect to knowing the will of God is to do with things beyond the written Word of God – such as this book that I am writing now! The Lord has been telling me to write books for the past five years or so, and because He told me to write them I know that I can ask for the money to pay for the books. However, if I wrote a book which I was not commanded to write, then I would have no faith to ask God for finances and He would not be obliged to provide them. Therefore, I would not write a book without first making sure that He had told me to do so. Thus faith is produced to see the project through to a conclusion.

So it is with my international trips. I have travelled to about 40 countries in the last five years and continue to travel to new countries each year. However, I know that the

Lord spoke very clearly about each country before I asked
God for the money to go. Again, if God had not told me to go
then the money would not have come. It has cost in the
region of £25,000 in airfares alone plus hotels, taxis, meals
etc. The Lord keeps providing and so it gives me faith to keep
asking and believing. In fact, I hardly need to ask these
days! The money just comes now since I have proved myself
in this area. This is how faith works when we are outside the
written Word of God. You need to have a Word from
the Holy Spirit to produce faith in your heart and then the
courage to act upon it! Faith and courage go together!

We are now going to look at the step-by-step process of
praying the prayer of faith.

> *'And Jesus answering saith unto them, **Have faith in God.**
> **For verily I say unto you, That whosoever shall say unto**
> **this mountain, Be thou removed, and be thou cast into**
> **the sea; and shall not doubt in his heart, but shall**
> **believe that those things which he saith shall come to**
> **pass; he shall have whatsoever he saith. Therefore I say**
> **unto you, What things soever ye desire, when ye pray,**
> **believe that ye receive them, and ye shall have them.**
>
> And when ye stand praying, forgive, if ye have ought
> against any: that your Father also which is in heaven may
> forgive you your trespasses. **But if ye do not forgive,**
> **neither will your Father which is in heaven forgive**
> **your trespasses.'**   (Mark 11:22–26)

Also look at:

> *'And all things, whatsoever ye shall ask in prayer, believing,*
> *ye shall receive.'*   (Matthew 21:22)

> *'And whatsoever ye shall ask in my name, that will I do, that*
> *the Father may be glorified in the Son.'*   (John 14:13)

> *'Ye have not chosen me, but I have chosen you, and ordained*
> *you, that ye should go and bring forth fruit, and that your*

fruit should remain: that whatsoever ye shall ask of the Father in my name, he may give it you.'   (John 15:16)

'And in that day ye shall ask me nothing. Verily, verily, I say unto you, Whatsoever ye shall ask the Father in my name, he will give it you.'   (John 16:23)

Once we have established in our heart that it is the will of God for us to have something we then need to know how to pray and release it in the earth.

Step 1: Ask
*'Hitherto have ye asked nothing in my name: **ask**, and ye shall receive, that your joy may be full.'*   (John 16:24)

Step 2: Believe that you receive
*'Jesus said unto him, If thou canst believe, all things are possible to him that **believeth**.'*   (Mark 9:23)

Step 3: Praise Him for answering your prayer
*'Be careful for nothing; but in every thing by prayer and supplication with **thanksgiving** let your requests be made known unto God.'*   (Philippians 4:6)

Step 4: Patiently wait for the full manifestation
*'That ye be not slothful, but followers of them who through faith and **patience** inherit the promises.'*   (Hebrews 6:12)

Step 5: Be ready at all times to fight against all doubts and unbelief
*'Take heed, brethren, lest there be in any of you an evil heart of **unbelief**, in departing from the living God.'*

(Hebrews 3:12)

Step 6: Having done all, to stand!
*'Wherefore take unto you the whole armour of God, that ye may be able to withstand in the evil day, and having done all, to **stand**.'*   (Ephesians 6:13)

You will have to protect your prayers against the devil's lies at all times, until you become established in this kind of praying. One of the reasons why many 'try' to pray in faith and give up easily is because they are not taught to fight our real enemy, who always attacks our mind! Guard your mind at all times. That is why we need to be in the Word of God regularly to keep faith strong and to starve any unbelief. I like what a man of God used to say:

'Feed your faith and starve your doubts to death!'

This man did great things for God and had this motto on all his work. We would all accomplish much more if we followed the same thinking.

I would like to give you a few examples of how I use this kind of prayer regularly.

A Place to Park

Today's traffic seems to get worse and worse! There are more cars on the road today than ever before. I have learned to pray all the time when I am driving and particularly when parking my car. My wife and I will often pray before leaving the house for a parking place at church. Our church is right in the centre of the city and there are only a few places to park. When we remember to pray there is always a place. If we forget then there is no place! This is always the case!

Getting Out at a Road Junction

In England we drive on the left-hand side of the road and whenever we have to turn right we have to cross both lanes. Sometimes there is a constant stream of traffic coming from both directions. I have learnt to pray and ask for a gap for me to get out. It always works within seconds of me praying! I have even proved it to people by deliberately not praying and having to wait and then praying and a place opens up almost straight away!

You may think that this is trivial but it is not. This is where your faith grows and confidence comes for bigger and bigger things.

Praying for Your Family to Be Saved

I understood a long time ago from the following scripture that it was God's will for my family to be saved:

> *'Who shall tell thee words, whereby thou and all thy house shall be saved.'*   (Acts 11:14)

From this verse I prayed for each one of my family members to get saved a long time ago. I asked for their salvation and thanked God in faith for saving them. This does not stop me praying for other aspects such as people to witness to them, taking authority over things to stop them from accepting, intercession etc. However, my stand point is that they are saved by faith. I am not moved by the fact that they do not show any interest in the gospel at all. I believe for them and it has taken away all worries about them going to heaven. I take every opportunity to share Jesus with them but not to push it down their throats! This will only drive them away! We have to be patient. I have been waiting in faith and patience for nearly 20 years for my parents to get saved. They have heard Ruth and me preach but still show no interest in Jesus Christ. I am still standing in faith for them to come to know Jesus Christ. I praise God for their salvation but I do not pray for them to be saved. I have already done that years ago. I believe that God heard my prayer the first time and so I simply stand and praise Him.

I have been in prayer sometimes and asked God for anything else that I should pray for them. Once the Lord led me to pray for my dad who was away abroad on business to be witnessed to by a Christian businessman who he would listen to. It worked! When my dad got home from the trip he told me that a man had talked to him about God on a plane

and given him a book to read. Praise God. Even though we
are standing in faith there are still things that we can do.

How to Pray for a Job

First of all you simply ask the Father for the best job to suit
you personally. Then you begin praising Him for that job.
You then go out and look for it!

> *'But wilt thou know, O vain man, that **faith without works***
> ***is dead?'***   (James 2:20)

You are now going with a job instead of for a job. You
received your job as soon as you prayed! This is how faith
works. You will still have to be patient and tenacious before
the right job manifests. The reason that we can have total
faith in this respect is because God said in His Word:

> *'For even when we were with you, this we commanded you,*
> *that **if any would not work, neither should he eat.'***
>   (2 Thessalonians 3:10)

> *'Let him that stole steal no more: **but rather let him***
> ***labour, working with his hands the thing which is***
> ***good, that he may have to give to him that needeth.'***
>   (Ephesians 4:28)

Chapter 7

From Faith to Faith

Paul says,

> 'For therein is the righteousness of God revealed **from faith to faith:** as it is written, **The just shall live by faith.**'
> (Romans 1:17)

Psalm 37:23 says,

> '**The steps of a good man are ordered by the LORD: and he delighteth in his way.**'

The Christian life is a series or progression of taking steps of faith. Faith should grow as we develop in Christ Jesus. If you examine the life of Jesus Himself in His earthly walk you will notice that He was walking in what I like to call 'Absolute faith'. He is our example in every aspect of life but especially in the area of faith. What a man of faith He was! Jesus healed the sick with very few words. He raised the dead with such ease! He fed the four and five thousand people so casually. He never even said a word to turn the water into wine! What faith He had!

The Bible then says about us:

> '**He that saith he abideth in him ought himself also so to walk, even as he walked.**'
> (1 John 2:6)

*'For even hereunto were ye called: **because Christ also
suffered for us, leaving us an example, that ye should
follow his steps.'***   (1 Peter 2:21)

We are therefore told to do the same things that Jesus did!

*'Verily, verily, I say unto you, He that believeth on me,
the works that I do shall he do also; and greater works
than these shall he do; because I go unto my Father.'*
(John 14:12)

That verse takes some faith!

When I first read this verse I could not believe it! I was so
amazed that I had to read it three or four times to see if it
actually meant what I thought it did. It did! I have sought to
believe to have that kind of faith and still have a quest to live
at that level of faith. I am not there yet but I am growing all
the time. My faith can only get stronger!

I am glad that my Father encourages me every so often by
telling me things like He told me last year. He said to me that
this year I would begin to see a real breakthrough in mighty
miracles of healing. This year is nearly over and I can say that
that word has come to pass. I have seen some wonderful
healings and miracles this year. To God be all the glory.

We go through seasons in our faith development. I know
that I do! I often feel as if I am being prepared in my faith for
another level – like a mini-wilderness. Then I find myself
doing great exploits in faith and I stand back in awe and just
praise God!

One of the areas in the lives of Ruth and myself in which
we have had to grow much in faith is the financial area.
When we first married we had to believe God for money
every week. This was tremendous training ground. I am
personally very grateful to God that He did it that way with
me. I say this because I am now in the position where I can
believe Him for any amount of money! We used to pray in
faith for £20 or £50 and it would come in. This really
encouraged our small faith. Then I can remember when we

had to pray for £100. It was a real hurdle but we got over it. Now we have to believe for thousands and tens of thousands regularly and it is the same way as before. The figures have just become larger all the time.

Ruth and I are so used to people coming up to us and giving us money that it has become a part of our lives. My faith in the financial realm is very high indeed and I never worry about where the next few thousand is coming from. I know it is on its way and I don't have to remind everyone that I meet either! I am sure that you have met that kind of person! Neither do I send out begging letters. That is not faith! If God is calling you to do something then He will provide the finances for it when the time is right. All you have to do is pray in faith, sow your seeds accordingly and stand in patience.

I have mentioned something here about sowing seeds in the financial area. I have written a book called *What the Bible Says About Your Provision and Prosperity*. This book will help you in every area of your financial decisions. Please contact the address at the back regarding our other books and ministry helps.

Basically, if you need £1000 then, provided that you are tithing to your local church, sow £10 into your church and believe for a one hundred-fold return which produces £1000. I do this all the time for airfares, books, etc. Ruth and I do this with household items as well and every time we need to buy something for the house we always have the money because we have sowed the seed.

We did it with our cars. Ruth and I have bought two cars over the last 12 months and paid cash for both! We did it by praying in faith for the car that we wanted (a Volvo) then we sowed a seed and named it for a car and then we stood in faith. We now have two wonderful cars debt free! In fact, if you did not know it yet, we live totally debt free in every aspect of our personal life, church, book publication and international travelling. We pay everything up front which means that we are the head and not the tail!

> *'The LORD shall open unto thee his good treasure, the heaven to give the rain unto thy land in his season, and to bless all the work of thine hand: and thou shalt lend unto many nations, and thou shalt not borrow. And the LORD shall make thee the head, and not the tail; and thou shalt be above only, and thou shalt not be beneath; if that thou hearken unto the commandments of the LORD thy God, which I command thee this day, to observe and to do them.'*
> (Deuteronomy 28:12–13)

This way of living removes all the worry that the world goes through in the financial area.

Your faith has to stand the test of time in every area of life. If faith has not been tested then if ever you come to a point where you need faith it seems like an insurmountable problem. But if you have gone from faith to faith one step at a time you will be able to overcome any mountain when you come to it.

I have seen situations where this is true. For example, I remember when I was in a major Pentecostal denomination in England and one of the top leaders had just retired from a position. His car, which came with that position, went as well and he did not know what to do. He had had a good income for many years with no worries and then his circumstances changed. He had no faith to believe that God could provide him with a car. This is so sad. This is why I believe that it is good for all people in ministry to have to be in a situation where they have to believe God in the financial realm so that when circumstances change they know how to trust in God.

> *'Charge them that are rich in this world, that they be not highminded, nor trust in uncertain riches, but in the living God, who giveth us richly all things to enjoy.'*
> (1 Timothy 6:17)

I am glad that Ruth and I have had to stand in faith for our daily food many times. We have often faced a month where we had no money at all. All we could depend on was God. We tell nobody when we need money since the Lord knows all about it.

> *'I have been young, and now am old; yet have I not seen the righteous forsaken, nor his seed begging bread.'* (Psalm 37:25)

Ruth and I have used this verse so many times!

> *'But thou, when thou prayest, enter into thy closet, and when thou hast shut thy door, pray to thy Father which is in secret; and thy Father which seeth in secret shall reward thee openly.'* (Matthew 6:6)

I would say that it has been the greatest way to develop my faith to have to constantly trust God for our daily needs.

What to Do When You Have No Money

When you are faced with this situation it is so easy to give in to pressure and take out a loan, overdraft or simply tell someone. This does not develop your faith in God and His Word.

I can remember when someone bought me a car many years ago. We had been standing in faith for a new car for about 11 months. The car finally came but we had to insure it! It cost me a whole month's salary! I said to Ruth that we could not buy any food or petrol or anything for 33 days. We simply went about our business and trusted God to provide for us. We got through and lived like kings! Money started to come in from all over the place! We lived as though I had a bottomless supply!

I remember another time when we had invited a friend to come and stay with us who had just been involved in a train crash. We had no money at all when we invited her to stay with us. She arrived and we said nothing. We could not go to the shops to buy food for her or us. I had hardly any fuel in my car also. The other factor is that we knew that she did not have any obvious means either. When she arrived she said that she wanted to take us to the supermarket. When we arrived she announced to us that we could buy all the food that we wanted and also clothes for the children. The reason why these things don't happen to many people is that they do not stand long enough. They give in too easily to the pressure. Faith has to be put under pressure!

Let's look at the account of Shadrach, Meshach, and Abednego in Daniel 3:17–28:

> 'If it be so, our God whom we serve is able to deliver us from the burning fiery furnace, and he will deliver us out of thine hand, O king. But if not, be it known unto thee, O king, that we will not serve thy gods, nor worship the golden image which thou hast set up.
>
> Then was Nebuchadnezzar full of fury, and the form of his visage was changed against Shadrach, Meshach, and Abednego: therefore he spake, and **commanded that they should heat the furnace one seven times more than it was wont to be heated**. And he commanded the most mighty men that were in his army to bind Shadrach, Meshach, and Abednego, and to **cast them into the burning fiery furnace**. Then these men were bound in their coats, their hosen, and their hats, and their other garments, and were cast into the midst of the burning fiery furnace. **Therefore because the king's commandment was urgent, and the furnace exceeding hot, the flame of the fire slew those men that took up Shadrach, Meshach, and Abednego**. And these three men, Shadrach, Meshach, and Abednego, fell down bound into the midst of the burning fiery furnace.
>
> Then Nebuchadnezzar the king was astonied, and rose up in haste, and spake, and said unto his counsellors, Did not we cast three men **BOUND** into the midst of the fire? They answered and said unto the king, True, O king. **He answered and said, Lo, I see four men LOOSE, walking**

*in the midst of the fire, and they have no hurt; and the
form of the fourth is like the Son of God.*

*Then Nebuchadnezzar came near to the mouth of the
burning fiery furnace, and spake, and said, Shadrach,
Meshach, and Abednego, ye servants of the most high God,
come forth, and come hither. Then Shadrach, Meshach, and
Abednego, came forth of the midst of the fire.*

*And the princes, governors, and captains, and the
king's counsellors, being gathered together, saw these
men, upon whose bodies the fire had no power, nor
was an hair of their head singed, neither were their
coats changed, nor the smell of fire had passed on
them.*

*Then Nebuchadnezzar spake, and said, Blessed be
the God of Shadrach, Meshach, and Abednego, who
hath sent his angel, and delivered his servants that
trusted in him, and have changed the king's word, and
yielded their bodies, that they might not serve nor
worship any god, except their own God.'*

This story always challenges me to the point that I wonder
where my faith would be if I was faced with this kind of
pressure! Jesus Himself showed up and delivered His precious
servants because they would not compromise the Word of
God.

Another situation is that of Joshua and Caleb. Look at what
happened with them because they dared to believe the Word
of God:

*'And Caleb stilled the people before Moses, and said,
Let us go up at once, and possess it; for we are well able
to overcome it.*

*And all the children of Israel murmured against Moses and
against Aaron: and the whole congregation said unto them,
Would God that we had died in the land of Egypt! or would
God we had died in this wilderness! And wherefore hath the
LORD brought us unto this land, to fall by the sword, that our
wives and our children should be a prey? were it not better for*

us to return into Egypt? And they said one to another, Let us make a captain, and let us return into Egypt.

Then Moses and Aaron fell on their faces before all the assembly of the congregation of the children of Israel. And Joshua the son of Nun, and Caleb the son of Jephunneh, which were of them that searched the land, rent their clothes: And they spake unto all the company of the children of Israel, saying, The land, which we passed through to search it, is an exceeding good land.

If the Lord delight in us, then he will bring us into this land, and give it us; a land which floweth with milk and honey. Only rebel not ye against the Lord, neither fear ye the people of the land; for they are bread for us: their defence is departed from them, and the Lord is with us: fear them not.

But all the congregation bade stone them with stones. And the glory of the Lord appeared in the tabernacle of the congregation before all the children of Israel. *And the Lord said unto Moses, How long will this people provoke me? and how long will it be ere they believe me, for all the signs which I have shewed among them?'*

(Numbers 13:30 & 14:2–11)

This is what happens every time we stand our ground to believe His Word. He shows up on our behalf and defeats all of our enemies and promotes us as well! Thus if you want your faith to keep growing you will have to go through greater trials of faith! It is that simple. I am doing things now that I used to read about in books and think that I could never do those things, because my faith level used to do somersaults! I would tremble at the thought of me ever doing anything remotely like what others were doing. Now I find myself in situations where I have to see God work a miracle and I hardly even think about it now.

I remember my first trip to Australia. I went with Peter Watkins and we went via Singapore and stayed there for five days. I felt that the Lord wanted us to stop there and so we did. This meant further expenses as usual! We had to have five nights in Singapore and seven nights in Sydney. I was then going on to Tasmania and Peter was flying home.

We arrived in the very humid heat in Singapore and found a hotel. I had very little money with me and so I needed a miracle! We rested the first day and then we made a telephone call to someone in the Full Gospel Businessmen's Fellowship. Peter made the contact and introduced me to the lady. I was asked to speak that night much to my pleasant surprise!

We went to speak at a house meeting (Methodist) and the people were very kind to us. However, they gave us no offering! We did not mention anything. Another lady said that she would take us the following day to another meeting that was full gospel. We went to another house group and we had awesome miracles, and they gave Peter and me an offering. It was a start! We ended up speaking five times in five days. On the Sunday we had been invited to go to a church service where they already had a speaker. I love the way God uses situations to really stretch my faith! I felt that we should go there but in the natural I could not possibly be the speaker and hence lost my last chance of an offering. I was still short of the money needed for Singapore let alone Sydney for seven nights!

We arrived in the meeting and it was full. There were pastors from many countries there besides us. The pastor asked me if I would speak for just five minutes. I began to give a prophetic word for the church and said that it would take longer than five minutes but I stopped after my five minutes were over. The visiting speaker motioned to the pastor that he did not want to speak but felt that I should speak. The pastor agreed and so I ended up taking the whole meeting! I spoke for about an hour and a half, prayed for the pastors, prophesied over people etc. Then the pastor took up an offering for us and the money was enough to pay for the rest of our time in Singapore and also Sydney! I left Sydney for Tasmania with just two Australian dollars (about £1 in those days). God is so good.

My faith has been through the fire over the years to be able to do such things and come out on top. I get so excited to see how God does it the next time. It is different every time! My faith continues to grow from faith to faith and I am ready for the next challenge!

Chapter 8

A Faith That Gives

'I have shewed you all things, how that so labouring ye ought to support the weak, and to remember the words of the Lord Jesus, how he said, It is more blessed to give than to receive.' (Acts 20:35)

*'For God so loved the world, that he **gave** his only begotten Son, that whosoever believeth in him should not perish, but have everlasting life.'* (John 3:16)

The world operates on a mentality of **how can I *get?*** But as Christians we should be always thinking the opposite – **how can I *give?***

If we are going to grow to maturity then we need to grow in this whole area of giving. God **so** loved that He gave! We should have the same attitude and be always on the look out to give into good ground. If you put a seed onto the road it will not produce a harvest but will die! A seed has to be in the right environment to grow and produce a harvest. I am very careful about sowing seeds these days and I am now going to help you to understand about good ground for your seeds.

Tithing

If you are reading this book and are not attending a local church then you are out of the will of God! You need to be in a church even if you do not agree with everything they say. It is scriptural!

> *'Not forsaking the assembling of ourselves together, as the manner of some is; but exhorting one another: and so much the more, as ye see the day approaching.'*
>
> (Hebrews 10:25)

> *'Abide in me, and I in you. As the branch cannot bear fruit of itself, except it abide in the vine; no more can ye, except ye abide in me.'*   (John 15:4)

> *'Obey them that have the rule over you, and submit yourselves: for they watch for your souls, as they that must give account, that they may do it with joy, and not with grief: for that is unprofitable for you.'*
>
> (Hebrews 13:17)

These verses speak for themselves. Who is going to give an account for your life? Leaders have this responsibility!

Thus we need to bring all of our tithes into the local church.

> *'Will a man rob God? Yet ye have robbed me. But ye say, Wherein have we robbed thee? In tithes and offerings. Ye are cursed with a curse: for ye have robbed me, even this whole nation.* **Bring ye all the tithes into the storehouse, that there may be meat in mine house, and prove me now herewith, saith the LORD of hosts, if I will not open you the windows of heaven, and pour you out a blessing, that there shall not be room enough to receive it. And I will rebuke the devourer for your sakes, and he shall not destroy the fruits of your ground; neither shall your vine cast her fruit before the time in the field, saith the LORD of hosts.** *And all nations shall call you blessed: for ye shall be a delightsome land, saith the LORD of hosts.'*
>
> (Malachi 3:8–12)

This is before we can really start giving to anyone. The church is the first place for all our giving! The tithe is holy unto the Lord!

> *'And all the tithe of the land, whether of the seed of the land, or of the fruit of the tree, is the LORD's: it is holy unto the LORD.'*   (Leviticus 27:30)

If you don't tithe then you are stealing from God according to these verses! That is serious! I am amazed how generous people are with visiting speakers and yet not to their own church. You will not prosper if that is you. The good news is that we can change! Start tithing now and pay back to your local church all the tithes that you owe it! One other point on tithing. If you are not confident to give your tithes to your church then you are in the wrong church. Find a church where you are confident about giving.

Look at this verse:

> *'For where your treasure is, there will your heart be also.'*   (Matthew 6:21)

If your heart is in something then your money will follow easily! It is a fact of life. Now that we have put all that straight we are in a position to give.

If we are believing for something then we sow a seed and name that seed. I am talking about our personal lives now. We always sow all of our seeds into our own local church in Hanley, Stoke-on-Trent. That is awesome ground for many reasons. Firstly, it is debt-free ministry. Never sow seeds into ministries that have any debt. Why should your good seeds be used to pay off somebody's bad management? Secondly, I know that everything that the church is doing is in line with the will of God. Also, we have proved again and again that our own financial situation just gets better and better as we keep sowing into our own church. There is an awesome anointing upon our church in the financial area which keeps growing all the time.

Where else should we be giving?

> *'But whoso hath this world's good, and seeth his brother*
> *have need, and shutteth up his bowels of compassion from*
> *him, how dwelleth the love of God in him?'*   (1 John 3:17)

This happens all the time in our church. If you know that someone has a need that you are able to help with then you do not need a prompting from God! Just do it. However, you need to be making sure that you are not funding someone's problem! That means that if that person thinks that they can simply live off soft Christians without working etc. then that is not good ground. Or if someone is smoking, drinking or taking drugs it is not right to keep helping them to kill themselves! Buy them some food or clothes but don't fund their bad habits. There are enough genuine needs around without wasting our godly substance.

The aspect of good ground is when the Lord specifically speaks to you about giving to someone. This is supernatural giving and usually causes the fastest harvests. This has happened to me many times. The Lord will speak to me about giving to someone and it often coincides with my own situation meaning that I am usually believing for something myself. This year I was in a situation where I was standing in faith for my new car. I had another car that I was going to use to trade in against mine. However, I decided to give it to someone in our church who did not have a car at all. I knew that they were standing for a car and so I gave them it and continued to stand for mine. Within four weeks of giving my car away I had my car paid for which was worth 13 times the car that I gave away! My old car became a seed.

We have done this many times. I have often been praying about something and asking God for something and He has said to give a seed in faith. This happened last year. I wanted a new camera and so I gave away my old one in faith. I was then in a position to buy my dream camera within about a week!

Praise God! We need to be seed minded not need minded. If you have a need then sow a seed! It works!

Chapter 9

Nothing to Fall Back On!

I have often thought of faith in God as a ship. When the ship is in the harbour it has plenty to anchor on to. The anchor itself has no problems getting to the bottom since the water is shallow. Also, the ropes can be tied easily onto the moorings. However, the further out the ship gets into the open sea it has less and less to depend upon. If it is close to the shores and a storm develops then it can fairly easily get back in time before trouble can occur. But if the ship is far out at sea with no land for miles then it has to weather the storm whatever the cost!

So it is with faith. When we first start out on this wonderful adventure of walking by faith we are often putting things to the test to see if it works. Then, as our confidence develops, we become more and more adventurous and bold.

Absolute faith is when we have nothing else to hold onto, just our faith and trust in God alone! I know that the Lord has been causing me to grow to this stage for a while now so that we are not relying on anything else but Him. This must surely be the goal for us all whatever our calling is in the Body of Christ.

Having said this, we must be ever aware that the Lord is dealing with us all at our different levels of faith and we must never become discouraged by measuring our level of faith with someone else who is way beyond us.

I once went to a conference abroad and saw the vision of a mighty man of God whom I look up to very much. He had accomplished so much that I felt so inadequate and that my measly contribution to Christianity was so insignificant in comparison. The Lord drew near to me and gave me these words that I shall never forget:

> 'Son, the only difference between you and him is 10 years.'

I was stunned to silence (which is a miracle!) as I thought on those words. The simple fact was that this minister had been going for 10 years longer than I, and I was simply 10 years behind him. In simple terms God was telling me that I would have the same kind of success as this man if I kept obeying everything that he was doing. I was so encouraged! I also asked the Lord why he had had so much success and His answer was very simple:

> 'He has done everything that I have told him to do.'

I know that if I continue doing everything that God tells me then our ministry will have the same kind of influence as him in a different way. I realise that God calls us all to do something different and no two ministries are ever the same.

The Transition from Believing to Knowing

A number of years ago I realised that faith is more than just believing! It is one thing to say that 'I believe in God' and another to say 'I know God'. For many years I believed God for healing and often stood in faith before the manifestation came. Then I moved from believing to knowing that I was healed! 1 Peter 2:24 says,

> *'Who his own self bare our sins in his own body on the tree, that we, being dead to sins, should live unto righteousness: by whose stripes ye were healed.'*

I thank God for my healing regularly since it is past tense! I know I am healed for the rest of my life.

Also for many years I struggled with the financial side of life. I was at the believing stage. I was always believing God for money for the ministry or our own personal life. This did us a lot of good because we were always seeking the Lord for something! It was motivating to stay close to the Lord. I know that there is a danger when Christians get on easy street and they are financially well off to drift away from having to trust God like they used to! Be warned! God had to warn Israel about this also!

> *'Beware that thou forget not the LORD thy God, in not keeping his commandments, and his judgments, and his statutes, which I command thee this day.'*   (Deuteronomy 8:11)

> *'But thou shalt remember the LORD thy God: for it is he that giveth thee power to get wealth, that he may establish his covenant which he sware unto thy fathers, as it is this day.'* (Deuteronomy 8:18)

Ruth and I are now in the knowing stage in the financial area. We have stood for years believing for things and have always been behind. Now we are ahead! I know that God has already provided everything for me to fulfil His call upon my life and also us as a family.

In fact, He spoke to me about two years ago and said this to me:

> 'You will never have to struggle again for money ... it will always be there.'

I can testify that in the last two years every time I have had a need for money it has been there for everything! We have also sown our seeds and named them all. (I refer you to my book, *What the Bible Says About Your Provision and Prosperity*, which you can order from the address at the back of this book.)

I know the Lord will provide and prosper me in every area of life as long as I continue doing His perfect will. I don't **believe** for finance any more as I **know** it will always come.

Ruth and I have been standing in faith for our own house for many years now, debt free. I know that I have it! It is not a struggle at all! I have moved from believing for a house to knowing that I have one.

The only time I have struggled to believe God was when He told me to ask for my own private jet! I was not expecting it. For two weeks I was in unbelief! I did not believe that God would do it for me. I knew that God could do it. That was not a problem. But for me to own a private jet for the ministry was too much for even my faith. The Lord spoke to me after the two weeks and rebuked me for not believing His word to my heart. I repented and then took the word very seriously and I am now in a state of faith for a jet. I even have a picture on the wall in my office! As I stood with Ruth and the children and our ministry about the jet I have noticed that my faith has increased regarding it. I know that I am moving from believing to **knowing** it is mine.

Some people call this the 'incubation period'. You become pregnant with something and then the vision is realised! This is how faith works.

I don't believe that I am saved ... I **know** I am saved!

I don't believe that I am healed ... I **know** I am healed!

I don't believe I am protected ... I **know** it!

This only comes with time as you continue in the Word of God and put it into practice every day. My faith in God is such that He can tell me anything and I will do it. I am now out on the open sea with nothing else to hold on to – only Him. Hallelujah!

Meditate on the following scriptures:

> *'They that go down to the sea in ships, that do business in great waters.'*   (Psalm 107:23)

> *'These see the works of the L*ORD*, and his wonders in the deep.'*   (Psalm 107:24)

*'Now when he had left speaking, he said unto Simon, **Launch out into the deep**, and let down your nets for a draught.'* (Luke 5:4)

*'**Deep calleth unto deep** at the noise of thy waterspouts: all thy waves and thy billows are gone over me.'* (Psalm 42:7)

How deep are you prepared to go in your faith and trust in the Lord? He is calling you to go deeper where you have never been before. It is exciting! He will never let you drown! I challenge you to become a deep water Christian for Jesus!

Chapter 10

Abraham

Abraham is mentioned much in the New Testament and is often referred to as 'The Friend of God'. However, we must always remember that the New Testament represents grace when it comes to making mention of Old Testament situations. If we only had the New Testament account of the life of Abraham to base our faith on then none of us would stand a chance! I am so glad that we have the full story!

Abraham demonstrated the same weaknesses that we all have to deal with, but he came through in the end as a champion of faith. The name of Abraham is mentioned all over the world today by millions of people because of his ultimate faith and faithfulness to the Lord.

We are now going to go on a journey from the beginning of God's dealings with him and realise that God is very patient with us, and is often more determined to fulfil His purpose through us than even we are ourselves! Genesis 12:1 says:

> 'Now the LORD had said unto Abram, Get thee out of thy country, and from thy kindred, and from thy father's house, unto a land that I will shew thee.'

The Lord told him to do this when Abraham was 70 years old in Ur of the Chaldees. However, Abraham waited until his father had died before he obeyed! This was five years later! Thus he delayed to obey the word of the Lord.

Also, God told him not to take any of his family with him. What did Abraham do? He took Lot with him which caused all kinds of problems for him! If you only had the New Testament to read then you would think that Abraham never ever made any mistakes. This is a source of comfort for all of us!

Notice that God never gave up on Abraham and He will not give up on us either as we keep seeking to do His work. One day we will have learnt all our lessons and be in a place where God can really use us to the full.

Eventually Abraham obeyed and went out in faith into a land that God would show him:

> *'And I will make of thee a great nation, and I will bless thee, and make thy name great; and thou shalt be a blessing: And I will bless them that bless thee, and curse him that curseth thee: and in thee shall all families of the earth be blessed. So Abram departed, as the LORD had spoken unto him; and Lot went with him: and Abram was seventy and five years old when he departed out of Haran.'*   (Genesis 12:2–4)

If you read this portion of Scripture quickly you would probably not realise that Abraham had delayed by five years and also disobeyed God's Word by taking Lot with him. Not a very good start for 'the father of faith'!

Throughout this adventure of faith God kept encouraging Abraham by appearing unto him. He did not have all the faith-building resources that we have today! No conventions to go to! No books to read or tapes to listen to!

Abraham then becomes afraid and tells lies to Pharaoh in Egypt about Sarai (Genesis 12:9–20).

During Abraham's travels he became very wealthy. However, so did Lot! This caused big problems between them and so they ended up parting company. I wonder if Abraham ever did realise that it was his fault that all this happened. The Bible does not tell us one way or the other. Greedy Lot chose the land that was good in the natural which almost cost him dearly! Sodom and Gomorrah was infested with evil of the worst kind. Homosexuality was rampant and all kinds of open sins. Lot did not know what he was letting himself in for!

These are the consequences when we disobey God. It pays to obey! Isaiah 1:19-20 says:

'If ye be willing and obedient, ye shall eat the good of the land: But if ye refuse and rebel, ye shall be devoured with the sword: for the mouth of the LORD hath spoken it.'

The Lord then promises Abraham a son from his own body and Abraham shows God that he believes it.

'And, behold, the word of the LORD came unto him, saying, This shall not be thine heir; but he that shall come forth out of thine own bowels shall be thine heir. And he brought him forth abroad, and said, Look now toward heaven, and tell the stars, if thou be able to number them: and he said unto him, So shall thy seed be. And he believed in the LORD; and he counted it to him for righteousness.'   (Genesis 15:4-6)

Abraham then makes the worst mistake of his life! Sarai encourages Abraham to have a child with her handmaid trying to fulfil the promise of God in the flesh!

'Now Sarai Abram's wife bare him no children: and she had an handmaid, an Egyptian, whose name was Hagar. And Sarai said unto Abram, Behold now, the LORD hath restrained me from bearing: I pray thee, go in unto my maid; ***it may be that I may obtain children by her.*** *And Abram hearkened to the voice of Sarai.'*   (Genesis 16:1-2)

Those three words ('it may be') should have been enough for Abraham to know that this was not from God at all. If ever you find yourself saying something like 'It may be', then remember this story! God does not need our help to fulfil His awesome plans! The Lord meant for Sarai to have a child by Abraham. Hagar produced Ishmael! Every time you turn to the arm of the flesh then you will produce an Ishmael!

One thing about 'Ishmaels' is that **they are very hard to get rid of**!

After this incident God was very quiet towards Abraham for a very long time. In fact God never spoke to him after that for a period of 13 years after Ishmael was born! I believe that The Lord was grieved with Abraham. I also believe that if Abraham had said no to Sarai and not gone with Hagar that he would have seen Isaac much sooner!

The Lord then rebukes Abraham so strongly that he falls on his face to the ground!

> *'And when Abram was ninety years old and nine, the LORD appeared to Abram, and said unto him, I am the Almighty God; walk before me, and be thou perfect. And I will make my covenant between me and thee, and will multiply thee exceedingly. And Abram fell on his face: and God talked with him, saying, As for me, behold, my covenant is with thee, and thou shalt be a father of many nations.'* (Genesis 17:1–4)

The Lord then did something most interesting with His servant. He changed his name from Abram to Abraham. He also changed Sarai's name to Sarah! God put an 'H' into both their names. The Lord did this for a reason. The name of God in the Hebrew language is unpronounceable in our English but is identified by the letter 'H'. What God was doing was to mingle His name with theirs in covenant. By this God was saying that all that belonged to Abraham was the Lord's and all that was the Lord's belonged to Abraham!

We shall now see something amazing! Even though God had said all this to Abraham and told him repeatedly that he would have a son with Sarah, he was still in unbelief about God's promise!

> *'Then Abraham fell upon his face, and laughed, and said in his heart, Shall a child be born unto him that is an hundred years old? and shall Sarah, that is ninety years old, bear? And Abraham said unto God, O that Ishmael might live before thee!'* (Genesis 17:17–18)

What a thing to say when God had made it abundantly clear about His purposes! It just goes to show how subtle unbelief can be!

In Genesis 18 we have the account of three angels visiting Abraham. God had to go to all this trouble all because of his unbelief. In fact if you read the passage very carefully you will realise that it is actually the Lord Himself who visits Abraham! Father, Son and Holy Spirit as three angels.

> *'And he lift up his eyes and looked, and, lo, three men stood by him: and when he saw them, he ran to meet them from the tent door, and bowed himself toward the ground, And said, My Lord, if now I have found favour in thy sight, pass not away, I pray thee, from thy servant.'*
>
> (Genesis 18:2–3)

> *'And they said unto him, Where is Sarah thy wife? And he said, Behold, in the tent. And he said, I will certainly return unto thee according to the time of life; and, lo, Sarah thy wife shall have a son. And Sarah heard it in the tent door, which was behind him.'*   (Genesis 18:9–10).

> *'And the LORD said unto Abraham, Wherefore did Sarah laugh, saying, Shall I of a surety bear a child, which am old? Is any thing too hard for the LORD? At the time appointed I will return unto thee, according to the time of life, and Sarah shall have a son.'*   (Genesis 18:13–14)

The Lord was still working on Abraham's faith to get him to believe the word. This is after 30 years! There is hope for you and me! Hallelujah!

Abraham then tells lies again because of Sarah through fear, and it was only through an act of God that Abimelech did not sleep with her. After all that Abraham had been through he was still acting unwisely! (Genesis 20).

Finally, Sarah conceives and Isaac is born. The consequences of Abraham's sin with Hagar quickly show up when Isaac is born because jealousy arises between Ishmael and Isaac, and Hagar and Ishmael end up having to leave. At last, Abraham and Sarah have their son of promise – but this is not the end of the story – read chapter 22!

The Lord calls upon Abraham to **sacrifice Isaac**!

Notice that Abraham did not tell Sarah what he was doing! I think that she would have done all within her power to dissuade Abraham from doing such a thing. Abraham had learned to keep his mouth shut and to just obey God!

The Word speaks for itself at this point:

> *'And they came to the place which God had told him of; and Abraham built an altar there, and laid the wood in order, and bound Isaac his son, and laid him on the altar upon the wood. And Abraham stretched forth his hand, and took the knife to slay his son. And the angel of the LORD called unto him out of heaven, and said, Abraham, Abraham: and he said, Here am I. And he said, Lay not thine hand upon the lad, neither do thou any thing unto him: for now I know that thou fearest God, seeing thou hast not withheld thy son, thine only son from me.'*   (Genesis 22:9–12)

It was a good job that Abraham was in the place where he heard and obeyed straight away or else Isaac would have died.

Also, it is important to fully realise what was going on in the mind of Abraham at this point. We need to read from the Book of Hebrews to fully understand why this was so significant.

> *'Accounting that God was able to raise him up, even from the dead; from whence also he received him in a figure.'*
>   (Hebrews 11:19).

Abraham's faith in God was now so strong that he actually believed that once he had killed Isaac with the knife and offered him up as a sacrifice by burning him on the altar, that he would then be raised up from the dead out of the ashes! Hallelujah!

No wonder that God Himself said, 'Now I know' in verse 12. Think about it!

Now I know, Abraham, that you will obey me whatever the cost.

Now I know that you will do what I say and go where I command!

Now I know that I can trust you absolutely in everything!

This was the moment that God had been waiting for with his servant for nearly 40 years of patient waiting!

Faith is a life-time's art! It takes time to develop. Just because your faith isn't where other people's is yet doesn't mean that it will never be. I used to read books about great men and women of faith who did great things for God and never ever thought that one day I would be doing similar things (and beyond!).

> *'The steps of a good man are ordered by the* Lord: *and he delighteth in his way. Though he fall, he shall not be utterly cast down: for the* Lord *upholdeth him with his hand.'*
>
> (Psalm 37:23–24)

Developing strong faith is really a series of many little steps until one day your faith is ready to move mountains!

God then says something awesome to Abraham:

> *'And said, By myself have I sworn, saith the* Lord, *for because thou hast done this thing, and hast not withheld thy son, thine only son:* **That in blessing I will bless thee, and in multiplying I will multiply thy seed as the stars of the heaven, and as the sand which is upon the sea shore; and thy seed shall possess the gate of his enemies.'***
>
> (Genesis 22:16–17)

Hallelujah! God finally has his man to fulfil His purpose through!

Now you can read about Abraham's faith in the New Testament and realise that it took many decades of stumbling around before he was ready.

'(As it is written, I have made thee a father of many nations,) before him whom he believed, even God, who quickeneth the dead, and calleth those things which be not as though they were. Who against hope believed in hope, that he might become the father of many nations; according to that which was spoken, So shall thy seed be.

And being not weak in faith, he considered not his own body now dead, when he was about an hundred years old, neither yet the deadness of Sarah's womb: He staggered not at the promise of God through unbelief; but was strong in faith, giving glory to God; And being fully persuaded that, what he had promised, he was able also to perform.' (Romans 4:17–21)

It took him a long time before he was fully persuaded!

This is the grace of God speaking. God does not hold against us our shortcomings and inadequacies, our unbelief and sin. Once we have grown up and repented of such things God forgets the past and launches us out into the arena to defeat the devil and see fruit that lasts for eternity! Glory to God!

Chapter 11

Faith That Turns Dreams Into Reality

'And Joseph dreamed a dream, and he told it his brethren: and they hated him yet the more. And he said unto them, Hear, I pray you, this dream which I have dreamed: For, behold, we were binding sheaves in the field, and, lo, my sheaf arose, and also stood upright; and, behold, your sheaves stood round about, and made obeisance to my sheaf.

And his brethren said to him, Shalt thou indeed reign over us? or shalt thou indeed have dominion over us? And they hated him yet the more for his dreams, and for his words. And he dreamed yet another dream, and told it his brethren, and said, Behold, I have dreamed a dream more; and, behold, the sun and the moon and the eleven stars made obeisance to me.

And he told it to his father, and to his brethren: and his father rebuked him, and said unto him, What is this dream that thou hast dreamed? Shall I and thy mother and thy brethren indeed come to bow down ourselves to thee to the earth? And his brethren envied him; but his father observed the saying.'   (Genesis 37:5–11)

I often think about this story and wonder what I would have said if I had dreamed such dreams! When I was a young man I would probably have told it to everyone just like

Joseph. Now I would almost certainly keep it to myself and perhaps one or two others whom I could trust totally. However, God's plan was realised even though Joseph did share it with his carnal brothers. God knew all the time that Joseph would share it and that his brothers would become even more jealous of him.

Joseph was his father's favourite son, which he made very obvious by giving him a coat of many colours. This action infuriated the rest of the family. A note here for all parents: don't ever show partiality with your children. Ruth and I have always sought to be absolutely equal in our dealings with our two wonderful children David and Joy. If we do something for one then we make it up to the other. This is so important. Jacob was not so sensible and reaped what he had sown for his bad decision. He was in heartache for a large part of his life because of it.

Joseph dreamed that he would one day be over his brothers and his father. He was almost the youngest apart from Benjamin. Such a dream was absurd in the natural, since the firstborn son used to have the birthright.

When the Lord gives us a word, dream or vision about the future it is usually hard to grasp. Also it never works out the way that we try to imagine with our finite minds. Remember that God is working on an eternal plan and we are just one piece of the gigantic jigsaw.

I remember when I was just 24 years old and speaking at a Pentecostal church in my own town in Stoke-on-Trent. I was pastoring in Salford at the time but had been invited to speak for a weekend and was staying at my parents' house. While I was alone in my bedroom I felt the presence of God come in and the Lord spoke to me about my calling. It was so supernatural. I did not share it for many years but kept it close to my heart. This calling has been confirmed over and again by different things but I never realised what it meant until recently, and I am about to celebrate my 40th birthday! Sixteen years of waiting and I am only just starting to see it unfold now. It is far bigger than I could ever have imagined. I have simply believed that one day it would come to pass.

Joseph was almost killed by his own brothers for sharing his dream but was delivered into a group of travellers called Ishmaelites who went into Egypt. They sold their own brother for a bit of silver and thought that that was the end of Joseph and his dreams! They then told lies to their father and said that a wild animal had killed him, and smeared his coat of many colours with animal blood and showed it to their father Jacob. This left poor Jacob in a sad state for many years and all of Joseph's brothers in guilt. They all resented Jacob because of the way that he treated Joseph and so Jacob never found out the real truth about Joseph until many years later.

Joseph went through all kinds of situations while in Egypt as a slave. He was falsely accused of attempted rape and thrown into prison as an innocent man. However, this was all to do with the process of refining Joseph, getting him ready for the ultimate calling upon his life. You see, before any of us can carry much responsibility we have to be rid of such things as arrogance, pride, ego, selfish ambition, greed etc. True humility is essential in any leadership responsibility.

Joseph was being prepared all the time, especially while in prison! What a humbling experience. He did not know that all this was his divine apprenticeship for the great work ahead.

Eventually, after a few false alarms (all part of the process) Joseph stood before Pharaoh and interpreted his dreams about the forthcoming time of plenty followed by a severe famine. Pharaoh decided to put Joseph in charge of stockpiling during the years of plenty so that there would be enough food during the famine. It is awesome to think that a Hebrew slave was given such a task! Only God could have done such a thing. Even during those seven years of plenty why should everyone believe him? It must have been God. Praise Him for evermore!

Joseph was finally in the place of destiny and ready to meet his brothers who had tried to kill him all those years ago! Would he mistreat them? He could even have had them killed. When they all arrived because of the famine Joseph decided to play some tricks on them to see what was in their hearts. Let us see what the Scripture says:

> *'And Joseph was the governor over the land, and he it was that sold to all the people of the land: and Joseph's brethren came, and bowed down themselves before him with their faces to the earth. And Joseph saw his brethren, and he knew them, but made himself strange unto them, and spake roughly unto them; and he said unto them, Whence come ye? And they said, From the land of Canaan to buy food. And Joseph knew his brethren, but they knew not him. And Joseph remembered the dreams which he dreamed of them, and said unto them, Ye are spies; to see the nakedness of the land ye are come.'* (Genesis 42:6–9)

Never in their wildest dreams could they have expected to see Joseph as head over Egypt! What a scene that must have been. I would love to have been a mosquito on the wall! Joseph must have begun to realise the importance of his dreams that he had so many years ago. It was not for ego's sake at all but God's love and compassion to keep His people alive in famine. They must have felt so ashamed when Joseph revealed himself to them!

> *'Then Joseph could not refrain himself before all them that stood by him; and he cried, Cause every man to go out from me. And there stood no man with him, while Joseph made himself known unto his brethren. And he wept aloud: and the Egyptians and the house of Pharaoh heard.*
>
> *And Joseph said unto his brethren, I am Joseph; doth my father yet live?* **And his brethren could not answer him; for they were troubled at his presence.** *And Joseph said unto his brethren, Come near to me, I pray you. And they came near.* **And he said, I am Joseph your brother, whom ye sold into Egypt. Now therefore be not grieved, nor angry with yourselves, that ye sold me hither: for God did send me before you to preserve life.**

> *For these two years hath the famine been in the land: and yet there are five years, in the which there shall neither be earing nor harvest. And God sent me before you to preserve you a posterity in the earth, and to save your lives by a great deliverance.'*
>
> (Genesis 45:1–7)

Joseph showed no hostility towards his brothers at all because **he understood by faith what God was doing!** In Genesis 50, Joseph makes this wonderful statement to his brothers:

> *'But as for you, ye thought evil against me; but **God meant it unto good, to bring to pass, as it is this day, to save much people alive.'***
>
> (Genesis 50:20)

If God gives you a dream, vision or word in your heart about the future then just keep a hold of it because one day it will come to pass. Never try to force it before the time, because all our efforts will be futile. Joseph tried this with the baker and butler and asked to be remembered and was forgotten for another two years!

> *'And the LORD answered me, and said, Write the vision, and make it plain upon tables, that he may run that readeth it. **For the vision is yet for an appointed time, but at the end it shall speak, and not lie: though it tarry, wait for it; because it will surely come, it will not tarry.'***
>
> (Habakkuk 2:2–3)

I believe that God is preparing all of us for His eternal purposes and as each one of us in the Body of Christ does his or her part then the whole will be accomplished. I am only responsible for doing what He commands me to do.

So keep your dreams and visions alive by faith because one day, just like Joseph, you will be standing in your dream with the right attitude free from all selfish motives, wrong thinking and self-gratification which will bring all the glory to Jesus Christ and God the Father. Praise God!

Chapter 12

Developing Consistent Faith

'Therefore, my beloved brethren, be ye stedfast, unmoveable, always abounding in the work of the Lord, forasmuch as ye know that your labour is not in vain in the Lord.'
(1 Corinthians 15:58)

'But the God of all grace, who hath called us unto his eternal glory by Christ Jesus, after that ye have suffered a while, make you perfect, stablish, strengthen, settle you.'
(1 Peter 5:10)

'And let us not be weary in well doing: for in due season we shall reap, if we faint not.' (Galatians 6:9)

When we look at God Himself we see the most consistent being. His creation demonstrates His absolute consistency in all things. The four seasons for instance shows His wonderful work. Since it is every Christian's desire to be like the Lord in everything, then we must set a goal at being consistent in our believing in all aspects of life. Herein lies the challenge. Life throws some interesting problems at us from time to time to try our faith. Look at this scripture:

'That the trial of your faith, being much more precious than of gold that perisheth, though it be tried with fire, might be

> *found unto praise and honour and glory at the appearing of*
> *Jesus Christ.'*   (1 Peter 1:7)

If we are to develop real, deep faith in God's Word then we will have to go through all kinds of trials. Faith isn't faith if it hasn't been tried! This is the only way to grow mature and strong in faith. Christians who are always up and down in their faith cannot be given any real responsibility in the kingdom. God is looking for people who will trust Him at all costs whatever happens to them.

Daniel was such a man! He put God first all the time and demonstrated consistency throughout his life. You may not realise it but Daniel was not in Jerusalem surrounded by fellow believers but in exile in a foreign country. The Jews were in captivity in a place called Babylon. Jerusalem had been invaded and Daniel had been taken. Daniel showed exceptional courage and faith throughout his lifetime and we would do well to remember his life when our going gets tough!

Daniel used to pray three times every day which was known by his enemies. It is interesting to note here that Daniel's consistency in prayer caused the enemy to launch an attack against him.

> *'Now when Daniel knew that the writing was signed, he went*
> *into his house; and his windows being open in his chamber*
> *toward Jerusalem, he kneeled upon his knees three times a*
> *day, and prayed, and gave thanks before his God, as he did*
> *aforetime. Then these men assembled, and found Daniel*
> *praying and making supplication before his God.'*
>   (Daniel 6:10–11)

They had Daniel thrown to the lions to try and get rid of him but their plan backfired!

> *'Then the king commanded, and they brought Daniel, and*
> *cast him into the den of lions. Now the king spake and said*
> *unto Daniel, Thy God whom thou servest continually, he will*
> *deliver thee. And a stone was brought, and laid upon the*

mouth of the den; and the king sealed it with his own signet, and with the signet of his lords; that the purpose might not be changed concerning Daniel. Then the king went to his palace, and passed the night fasting: neither were instruments of musick brought before him: and his sleep went from him.

Then the king arose very early in the morning, and went in haste unto the den of lions. And when he came to the den, he cried with a lamentable voice unto Daniel: and the king spake and said to Daniel, O Daniel, servant of the living God, is thy God, whom thou servest continually, able to deliver thee from the lions?

Then said Daniel unto the king, O king, live for ever. My God hath sent his angel, and hath shut the lions' mouths, that they have not hurt me: forasmuch as before him innocency was found in me; and also before thee, O king, have I done no hurt.' (Daniel 6:16–22)

Daniel wouldn't compromise his faith in God and the Lord brought about a great deliverance that ended up in Daniel being revered and promoted each time the enemy attacked him. This is the power of a consistent life. You keep bouncing back!

I had a situation in 1998 that challenged my consistency. We were having a healing service in our church and during the service a man walked into the meeting as if he came for healing. It was an invitation service and so we expected some new people. He came forward for prayer and I prayed for him. I then saw him leave just before the meeting finished. I assumed that he went down the stairs but he did not. Instead he went quietly into the office section of our building and into my office. My office was not locked at the time and he stole my laptop computer, stereo and the church's petty cash. After the service I went into my office for my traditional cup of coffee to wind down after ministry. I then noticed that all my stuff was gone. Any preacher knows that just after preaching we are at our most vulnerable. Preaching is very demanding, mentally, emotionally, physically and spiritu- ally all at the same time!

I was angry at what had happened and then my wife Ruth walked in and she was angry as well. Then the Lord spoke to me and told me to rejoice just like I would have counselled others to do! I tried to rejoice but was hurting inside. My praises were not getting through since I was so upset. I then asked God why this had happened and He said, 'The devil hates your books and is trying to slow them down.' I write all my books using a laptop computer.

The Lord then said to me 'Anyway the laptop computer that was stolen was getting old and I wanted you to have a new one!'. My countenance changed straight away and I told Ruth what God had just said to me. Incidentally, my old laptop was not insured since it costs a fortune to insure them.

Exactly three weeks later I was in Chicago preaching and all that time I was rejoicing and praising God for my new laptop. They cost about £1,600 for a new one.

I went that afternoon to look at laptops in the USA since they are cheaper over there and I wanted to price them up. I arrived back to the house where I was staying and the husband came home from work and found out that I was looking for a laptop. He came to me and asked me to go along to the computer store with him straight away. I told him that I had already been and had priced them up for some future date when I had the money to buy one. He said 'Come on, let's go.' I repeated myself and said that I did not have the money so it was a pointless exercise. He then said that he did not ask me if I had the money since he was going to buy me one! I stood in shock for a few minutes. I had never met this man before and he was going to casually buy me a laptop! We went to the store and there was a Compaq on special offer for just $2000. He bought it for me and also bought all the extras, spare battery for travelling, more memory, leather carry case etc. It was just the Lord!

That would be a great testimony if it ended there but there is more. The following day this man went to work and was due a bonus cheque. He was handed an extra bonus cheque for $40,000 out of the blue. Twenty times what he spent on my laptop! What the devil tried to do to slow me down has actually backfired and I am now writing four books a year instead of three!

Inconsistent people complain when everything doesn't go right with them all the time. Let me tell you that when you walk by faith you are going to have setbacks, trials, persecutions, difficulties and opportunities to give up. But those who endure the storms and develop a consistent faith will end up being continually promoted and fulfilling their destiny.

Take a look at this passage:

> *'Who passing through the valley of Baca make it a well; the rain also filleth the pools. They go from strength to strength, every one of them in Zion appeareth before God.'*
>
> (Psalm 84:6–7)

The valley of Baca can equally be translated as the valley of weeping. Notice it says that we pass through this valley of weeping. When we do we will go from strength to strength! However, some people start out well and have a problem in their life and they make their home in Baca! They moan, grumble and complain about that situation instead of passing through it. We all go through valleys of tears at times but faith believes that it will come to an end soon. All storms have an end!

One thing I have learnt about problems, difficulties etc. is that we learn more by having to use our faith than when everything is going well. One person said that we would never have a victory if we never had a fight!

> *'Fight the good fight of faith, lay hold on eternal life, whereunto thou art also called, and hast professed a good profession before many witnesses.'* (1 Timothy 6:12)

> *'Knowing this, that the trying of your faith worketh patience.'* (James 1:3)

> *'That ye be not slothful, but followers of them who through faith and patience inherit the promises.'* (Hebrews 6:12)

> *'And so, after he had patiently endured, he obtained the promise.'*
>   (Hebrews 6:15)

Notice that the word 'patience' keeps being mentioned alongside faith and trials. I have been pastoring people for 18 years now and I have observed that consistent people are patient people. Also, inconsistent people are impatient people. Faith and patience are married! If you are to develop consistent faith then you will have to get a revelation of patience along with joy. Joyful patience added to strong faith will cause you to be a champion!

Abraham was patient and his faith is still influencing the world thousands of years after his death! Joseph was patient and ended up delivering all of God's people from starvation. David had to be patient with Saul around even though he had been anointed by Samuel. Eventually the day came when David was king and what a king he was! David showed great consistency all through his life apart from twice when he made rash decisions. However, even though he made such terrible mistakes God did not write him off! The reason was that God knew David's heart and David repented and went on to be even stronger.

This brings us to another ingredient of faith: **faith never holds on to past failures**.

> *'Brethren, I count not myself to have apprehended: but this one thing I do, forgetting those things which are behind, and reaching forth unto those things which are before.'*
>   (Philippians 3:13)

Don't live life 'in the rear view mirror'. Look ahead. Repent of all sins and move on! **God isn't looking for sinless people**. He never has done because we have all sinned and need His mercy and grace. He is looking for those who get rid of sin and walk in holiness and purity! Keep on developing that winning attitude of faith, patience, joy and consistency and just watch how God will promote you!

Chapter 13

The Simple Faith of Jesus Christ!

When Jesus walked on the earth He talked much about faith and made many statements regarding the subject. He also demonstrated faith and made it all look so easy! Striving was never a part of His ministry – He simply touched people and they were miraculously healed. I don't know about you but I want that kind of simple trust that gets the job done every time I pray for anybody!

Spend some time simply meditating on the following scriptures:

> 'And Jesus rebuked the devil; and he departed out of him: and the child was cured from that very hour. Then came the disciples to Jesus apart, and said, Why could not we cast him out?
>
> And Jesus said unto them, Because of your unbelief: for verily I say unto you, If ye have faith as a grain of mustard seed, ye shall say unto this mountain, Remove hence to yonder place; and it shall remove; and nothing shall be impossible unto you. Howbeit this kind goeth not out but by prayer and fasting.' (Matthew 17:18–21)

> 'But Jesus beheld them, and said unto them, **With men this is impossible; but with God all things are possible**.'
> (Matthew 19:26)

'Jesus said unto him, If thou canst believe, all things are possible to him that believeth.'   (Mark 9:23)

'Wherefore, if God so clothe the grass of the field, which today is, and to morrow is cast into the oven, shall he not much more clothe you, O ye of little faith?.'

(Matthew 6:30)

'When Jesus heard it, he marvelled, and said to them that followed, Verily I say unto you, I have not found so great faith, no, not in Israel.'   (Matthew 8:10)

'And he saith unto them, Why are ye fearful, O ye of little faith? Then he arose, and rebuked the winds and the sea; and there was a great calm.'   (Matthew 8:26)

'But Jesus turned him about, and when he saw her, he said, Daughter, be of good comfort; thy faith hath made thee whole. And the woman was made whole from that hour.'

(Matthew 9:22)

'Then touched he their eyes, saying, According to your faith be it unto you.'   (Matthew 9:29)

'And immediately Jesus stretched forth his hand, and caught him, and said unto him, O thou of little faith, wherefore didst thou doubt?'   (Matthew 9:29)

Whenever Jesus was dealing with His disciples He was always trying to assist their believing and confronting their fears and worries. Even with Thomas He took the time to help him to see his doubt and get him into a place of faith. Notice that Jesus did this before doing anything else!

'But Thomas, one of the twelve, called Didymus, was not with them when Jesus came. The other disciples therefore said unto him, We have seen the Lord. But he said unto them, Except I shall see in his hands the print of the

nails, and put my finger into the print of the nails, and thrust my hand into his side, I will not believe.

*And after eight days again his disciples were within, and Thomas with them: then came Jesus, the doors being shut, and stood in the midst, and said, Peace be unto you. **Then saith he to Thomas, Reach hither thy finger, and behold my hands; and reach hither thy hand, and thrust it into my side: and be not faithless, but believing.** And Thomas answered and said unto him, My Lord and my God.*

Jesus saith unto him, Thomas, because thou hast seen me, thou hast believed: blessed are they that have not seen, and yet have believed.' (John 20:24–29)

This last statement by Jesus is awesome regarding faith! Just take some time to think about it. It is the highest level of faith simply to believe His word without seeing anything. This is what I have come to understand as **absolute faith!**

Just watch how this absolute faith works miracles:

'And when they wanted wine, the mother of Jesus saith unto him, They have no wine. Jesus saith unto her, Woman, what have I to do with thee? mine hour is not yet come. His mother saith unto the servants, Whatsoever he saith unto you, do it.

*And there were set there six waterpots of stone, after the manner of the purifying of the Jews, containing two or three firkins apiece. **Jesus saith unto them, Fill the waterpots with water.** And they filled them up to the brim. And he saith unto them, Draw out now, and bear unto the governor of the feast. And they bare it.'* (John 2:3–8)

What could be easier? Jesus did not even pray anything and the wine appeared!

The healing of the nobleman's son is just as simple.

'So Jesus came again into Cana of Galilee, where he made the water wine. And there was a certain nobleman, whose son was sick at Capernaum. When he heard that Jesus was

> come out of Judaea into Galilee, he went unto him, and
> besought him that he would come down, and heal his son:
> for he was at the point of death. Then said Jesus unto him,
> Except ye see signs and wonders, ye will not believe. The
> nobleman saith unto him, Sir, come down ere my child die.
>
> Jesus saith unto him, Go thy way; thy son liveth. And the
> man **believed** the word that Jesus had spoken unto him, **and
> he went his way.**
>
> And as he was now going down, his servants met him, and
> told him, saying, Thy son liveth. Then inquired he of them
> the hour when he began to amend. And they said unto him,
> Yesterday at the seventh hour the fever left him. **So the
> father knew that it was at the same hour, in the which
> Jesus said unto him, Thy son liveth: and himself
> believed, and his whole house.'**   (John 4:46–53)

Jesus hardly did anything with both these miracles and yet
it caused a revival with his whole house getting saved! Many
people ask the question regarding whether or not we can
perform the same miracles since we are only human? Let us
look at what Jesus said about this.

> 'Verily, verily, I say unto you, He that believeth on me, the
> works that I do shall he do also; and greater works than these
> shall he do; because I go unto my Father.'   (John 14:12)

What a statement – Jesus is inviting us to do exactly what
He did and more! He has a lot of faith in us doesn't He?

> 'And as ye go, preach, saying, The kingdom of heaven is at
> hand. Heal the sick, cleanse the lepers, raise the dead, cast
> out devils: freely ye have received, freely give.'
>
>   (Matthew 10:7–8)

Jesus said this to His disciples who later on deserted Him.
How much more do you think those of us who serve Him
with all our hearts should be seeing healing, deliverance and
miracles on a regular basis!

At the end of Mark's Gospel Jesus then says this to the whole Church:

> *'And these signs shall follow them that believe; In my name shall they cast out devils; they shall speak with new tongues; They shall take up serpents; and if they drink any deadly thing, it shall not hurt them; they shall lay hands on the sick, and they shall recover.'*   (Mark 16:17–18).

Let us all stop making excuses and start doing the works to glorify God. I know that we are not perfect. We all have to struggle with pride, ego, self-exaltation etc., but the Lord will deal with all that. The worst thing that you can do is to wait until all those things are dealt with! God works with our character 'on the job' so to speak! He is refining us all the time and there is always repentance! If you want strong faith then spend much quality time meditating on the Word of God because that is where faith develops. We then become confident as we start to act on it.

The very first time this happened to me was at university when I was 19 years old. I had only recently been born again and knew very little about anything when it came to spiritual things! One day I read that I could lay hands on the sick and they would recover! Nobody had ever told me that before and so I prayed a simple prayer to the Lord. 'Please Lord, send someone to me who is sick so that I can lay my hands on them'. That was in the morning in my quiet time with God. (This used to last about three hours when I was at university!)

In the evening a fellow student called Mark came into my room. He was complaining about a severe headache that he had had all day and could not do any studies. I said to him that I wanted to pray for him to be healed. He then said to me that he was an atheist and that he did not believe in God at all. I said 'No problem, I will do the believing for you!' What was I saying? I simply believed God's Word! He said that it couldn't possibly work since he did not believe in God. I persisted and he said 'OK'. I prayed a simple prayer of faith to tell the headache to go and he left my room. About

10 minutes later he came back to my room and said, 'My headache has gone!' Mark then came to church with me the next day and found Jesus Christ as his Lord and Saviour! Hallelujah! That was my introduction to the healing ministry. I have been praying for the sick now for 19 years and have since laid my hands on sick people in all six continents and seen hundreds of miracles.

I remember one day back in my pastoral days in Manchester. We were having a service on Sunday morning as usual and a lady came forward for healing. She was in her late sixties and wanted prayer for arthritis in her back. I asked her if she knew Jesus as her Saviour and she said 'no'. I then asked her if she wanted to be saved and she said '**no**.' She said that she was not interested in being born again. All she wanted was her healing! Her son came to our church and he had invited her. I prayed for her and she went down under the power of the Holy Spirit like a stone. She hit the ground with such a thump on her back where her condition was at its worst! She got up and hobbled back to her seat.

The following morning I was in prayer and the Lord spoke to me and said 'Go and visit that lady.' I obeyed and found her flat. She then told me the story! When she left the church she tried to find her way home but was so overcome by the power of God that she ended up in the wrong street! She said that it took her ages to find her flat. I then asked her again if she wanted to be saved and she said 'Yes please.' She had been completely healed and knew that only God could do that. She became a very faithful member in that church and went from faith to faith!

In 1997 I took a team of people from our church to India. We visited a church which was in a rural village miles from any city or town and we had a one night healing meeting. The pastor was expecting about a thousand people to come. When the meeting started there were 2,500 people crowding the hall, who were mostly Hindus. I preached a simple message of faith in God and healing in the name of Jesus Christ. When I gave the appeal for people to accept Jesus as Saviour there were 356 hands in the air who all got saved that night!

We then prayed for the sick but not by laying on of hands. I simply stretched my hand out across the huge crowd and spoke by word of knowledge. I rebuked sickness, disease and demons and many were healed instantly. Demons came out of hundreds to the glory of God. After the meeting the people thronged us as a team and begged us to lay our hands on them. We finally arrived back at our mud hut surrounded by a paddy field which was cobra infested. The pastor then told us in the morning that the people stayed for four hours after the service to testify about the miracles that had taken place. Many of the people stayed until two o'clock in the morning to tell what had happened to them. Hallelujah!

I have the hands ... He has the power! My job is to lay hands on or simply to speak the word and then leave the miracles up to God!

Chapter 14

Fasting and
Praying in the Spirit

These two ingredients are absolutely imperative if we are going to mature in our faith walk. The reason for this is that both these things are needed to tune our spirit in with the Holy Spirit.

One of the problems of living on earth is that there are many voices trying to take our attention away from the things of God. We often get so cluttered up with the things of this world that when God does try to speak to us we can't actually hear Him. This is why the Bible talks a lot about fasting because it tunes us in to the Spirit so well.

Take a look at these verses from Job:

> 'For God speaketh once, yea twice, yet man perceiveth it not. In a dream, in a vision of the night, when deep sleep falleth upon men, in slumberings upon the bed; Then he openeth the ears of men, and sealeth their instruction, That he may withdraw man from his purpose, and hide pride from man.'
> (Job 33:14–17)

As we step out in faith we also need to be ever aware that the Holy Spirit will want to guide our faith into the perfect will of God. Always listen to the voice of God in your believing and faith ventures or else it will end up your purposes and not His. Praying in the Holy Spirit helps us, along with fasting, to enable our faith to work at the maximum level.

> *'But ye, beloved, building up yourselves on your most holy faith, praying in the Holy Ghost.'* (Jude 1:20)

> *'Likewise the Spirit also helpeth our infirmities: for we know not what we should pray for as we ought: but the Spirit itself maketh intercession for us with groanings which cannot be uttered. And he that searcheth the hearts knoweth what is the mind of the Spirit, because he maketh intercession for the saints according to the will of God.'* (Romans 8:26–27)

During my 18 years of full-time ministry I have spent much time praying in the Spirit along with fasting. In fact for many years I fasted for two to three days every week. At the moment I am in the middle of my longest fast of 21 days with just liquids. I have never done such a long fast before but felt the Holy Spirit prompting me to do so in preparation for my 40th birthday. I must admit that it has been much easier than I thought it would be! I have drunk twice as much as normal, which I feel is common sense, and am now starting to feel fairly weak in my body after 15 days. However, my mind and spirit are very active and full of life.

Read through Isaiah 58 and see all the many reasons given for fasting. Also note that Jesus went on a 40-day fast prior to ministry as did Moses to get the Ten Commandments.

I decided a long time ago that since God had given me a deliverance ministry I needed to be in touch with the Holy Spirit and so I have fasted and prayed very much to maintain a close walk with God and to hear accurately what He wants to say. I find it easy now to hear from God since my spirit is tuned in this way. This causes faith to work at its best!

> *'Howbeit this kind goeth not out but by prayer and fasting.'* (Matthew 17:21)

Peter also tells us things that we need to add to our faith to make sure that we remain rock solid:

> *'And beside this, giving all diligence, add to your faith virtue; and to virtue knowledge; And to knowledge temperance; and to temperance patience; and to patience godliness; And to godliness brotherly kindness; and to brotherly kindness charity. For if these things be in you, and abound, they make you that ye shall neither be barren nor unfruitful in the knowledge of our Lord Jesus Christ.'*   (2 Peter 1:5–8)

Paul also speaks about another ingredient!

> *'And though I have the gift of prophecy, and understand all mysteries, and all knowledge;* **and though I have all faith, so that I could remove mountains, and have not charity, I am nothing.**
>
> *Charity suffereth long, and is kind; charity envieth not; charity vaunteth not itself, is not puffed up, Doth not behave itself unseemly, seeketh not her own, is not easily provoked, thinketh no evil; Rejoiceth not in iniquity, but rejoiceth in the truth; Beareth all things, believeth all things, hopeth all things, endureth all things.*
>
> *Charity never faileth: but whether there be prophecies, they shall fail; whether there be tongues, they shall cease; whether there be knowledge, it shall vanish away.'*
>
> (1 Corinthians 13:2, 4–8)

> *'For in Jesus Christ neither circumcision availeth any thing, nor uncircumcision; but* **faith which worketh by love.**'
>
> (Galatians 5:6)

The development of our Christian character is just as important as the growth of our faith. Honesty, truth and integrity need to grow as well as faith to move mountains.

> *'But speaking the truth in love,* **may grow up into him in all things**, *which is the head, even Christ.'*   (Ephesians 4:15)

Therefore, don't just concentrate on one area of your Christian development but on everything! A garden which has superb roses in one section and weeds everywhere else looks silly! So do we if the whole of our Christian character is not maintained.

Chapter 15

Faith for Revival

The greatest desire of my heart is to see a spiritual awakening in our country. I believe that the Bible promises a worldwide outpouring of the Holy Spirit before the end can come. Some countries have been experiencing awesome things in the last few years, which is a sign of revival. Let us look at some of the things the Word of God has to say about this:

> 'But as truly as I live, all the earth shall be filled with the glory of the LORD.' (Numbers 14:21)

> 'They shall not hurt nor destroy in all my holy mountain: for the earth shall be full of the knowledge of the LORD, as the waters cover the sea.' (Isaiah 11:9)

> **'For the earth shall be filled with the knowledge of the glory of the LORD, as the waters cover the sea.'**
> (Habakkuk 2:14)

> 'Sow to yourselves in righteousness, reap in mercy; break up your fallow ground: **for it is time to seek the LORD, till he come and rain righteousness upon you.'** (Hosea 10:12)

> 'Ask ye of the LORD rain in the time of the latter rain; so the LORD shall make bright clouds, and give them showers of rain, to every one grass in the field.' (Zechariah 10:1)

'And it shall come to pass afterward, that I will pour out my spirit upon all flesh; and your sons and your daughters shall prophesy, your old men shall dream dreams, your young men shall see visions.' (Joel 2:28)

We must all do what God calls us to in this revival and that means firstly that we are to believe for it! Some Christians are not in faith for revival at all. Well, you will never see what you don't believe for! Start to speak about it, which is general agreement with Scripture. Also, ask the Lord what your part is in the last day outpouring. You may get a surprise! He may call you to do something very specific to add to it! Just do what He says and the job will get done.

One of the things that was prophesied towards the end of the 1980s was that God would begin a new thing in Great Britain by raising up new churches in city centres all over the land. I did not hear about this prophecy until 1992 when we had already been going for about a year! God had called upon me to pioneer a new church and for it to be located right in the centre of Stoke-on-Trent. We now have nine churches across Britain with more in the pipeline. Revival is on its way and I am in the epicentre of it in my locality. Hallelujah!

Use your faith for revival above all else. It is a good thing to develop your faith by using it for cars, houses, holidays etc. but the faith in our heart is to see the kingdom of God established in our land! Don't become selfish with your faith. Start to believe God now for revival for your area and listen to what He would have you to do about it!

And lastly:

- Faith turns weaklings into warriors!
- Faith produces courage and conviction.
- Faith overcomes fear and worry.
- Faith looks forwards instead of backwards!
- Faith walks through fires and storms.
- Faith defeats Satan and all opposition.
- Faith says yes to impossibilities.

- Faith never gives up but marches onward.
- Faith casts mountains into the sea.
- Faith turns weaknesses into opportunities.
- Faith turns to flight the armies of the aliens.
- Faith hangs on to nothing but God and His Word.
- Faith transforms cowards into conquerors!
- Faith ignites hope and expectancy.
- Faith turns dreams into realities.

'Now faith is the substance of things hoped for, the evidence of things not seen.'   (Hebrews 11:1)

'Through faith we understand that the worlds were framed by the word of God, so that things which are seen were not made of things which do appear.'   (Hebrews 11:3)

'But without faith it is impossible to please him: for he that cometh to God must believe that he is, and that he is a rewarder of them that diligently seek him.'
                          (Hebrews 11:6)

'By faith Noah, being warned of God of things not seen as yet, moved with fear, prepared an ark to the saving of his house; by the which he condemned the world, and became heir of the righteousness which is by faith.'   (Hebrews 11:7)

'By faith the walls of Jericho fell down, after they were compassed about seven days. By faith the harlot Rahab perished not with them that believed not, when she had received the spies with peace.
And what shall I more say? for the time would fail me to tell of Gedeon, and of Barak, and of Samson, and of Jephthae; of David also, and Samuel, and of the prophets: **Who through faith subdued kingdoms, wrought right-eousness, obtained promises, stopped the mouths of lions, Quenched the violence of fire, escaped the edge of**

the sword, out of weakness were made strong, waxed valiant in fight, turned to flight the armies of the aliens.

Women received their dead raised to life again: and others were tortured, not accepting deliverance; that they might obtain a better resurrection: And others had trial of cruel mockings and scourgings, yea, moreover of bonds and imprisonment: They were stoned, they were sawn asunder, were tempted, were slain with the sword: they wandered about in sheepskins and goatskins; being destitute, afflicted, tormented.' (Hebrews 11:30–37)

*'Wherefore seeing we also are compassed about with so great a cloud of witnesses, let us lay aside every weight, and the sin which doth so easily beset us, and let us run with patience the race that is set before us, **Looking unto Jesus the author and finisher of our faith; who for the joy that was set before him endured the cross, despising the shame, and is set down at the right hand of the throne of God.'*** (Hebrews 12:1–2)

Jesus Christ Himself is both the author and finisher of our faith. This means the one who adds the finishing touches to our faith. It can also be translated 'perfecter'. The *Strong's Concordance* also says 'completer'. In other words, Jesus comes alongside us as we use our faith and helps to complete the tasks that He set for us in the first place. Hallelujah!

Other books by Trevor Newport

What the Bible says about YOUR Provision and Prosperity
Did you go OR were you sent? (An autobiography)
King Jesus is Coming Soon!
Angels, Demons and Spiritual Warfare
The Ministry of Jesus Christ
Divine Appointments
The Two U's: Unbelief and Unforgiveness
Secrets of Success
From Victory to Victory
Pitfalls in Ministry
How to Pray in the Spirit
The Anointing: the Vital Ingredient

For more information about any aspect of this ministry please contact:

Life-Changing Ministries
Bemersley House
Gitana Street
Hanley
Stoke-on-Trent
Staffordshire
ST1 1DY
England

Phone: 01782 272 671
(*overseas*: +44 1782 272 671)
Fax: 01782 274 411

Website: www.lcm.clara.net